FROM THE KIPPAH TO THE CROSS

Jean-Marie Élie Setbon

FROM THE KIPPAH TO THE CROSS

A Jew's Conversion to Catholicism

In collaboration with Astrid de Larminat

Translated by C. A. Thompson-Briggs

IGNATIUS PRESS   SAN FRANCISCO

Original French edition:
De la kippa à la Croix
© 2013 by Éditions Salvator, Paris
All rights reserved

Cover design/illustration by John Herreid

© 2015 by Ignatius Press, San Francisco
All rights reserved
ISBN: 978-1-62164-018-9
Library of Congress Control Number 2014959625
Printed in the United States of America ∞

*To the memory of all my Jewish brothers and sisters
who have taken the plunge into Christ,
and especially Jean-Marie Cardinal Lustiger,
Rabbi David Drach, François Libermann,
and Hermann Cohen*

To the memory of my mother

*To the memory of my first wife, Martine
To my wife, Pétronille*

*To my eight children: Rachel, Déborah, Rébecca,
Myriam, Raphaël, Gabriel, Louis, and Nathanaël*

To My Patron Saint

You, Saint John the Evangelist,
You who lay upon the heart of our God and Savior,
  Jesus,
You who were His beloved,
I put myself under your patronage, under your protection.

"John" means "God compassionate"
But in your name, there is also the word "grace", the grace
  divine.

Thus you, Saint John, who had that grace divine
  to lay upon the heart of God,
You who saw the Word and who proclaimed it to us,
You who were converted to Christ, to what He is and represents,
You who have given us
  the Gospel,
  the Letters,
  the Apocalypse,
Pray for me,
That I may be evermore a child of God,
That I may be evermore converted each day,
That I may become evermore your little brother,
That this book, which testifies to what Jesus has done and
  to what He continues to do in my life,
May touch the heart of each person who reads it.

Amen.

CONTENTS

PREFACE

Christ turned around Saint Paul, my dear travelling companion, in three days on the road to Damascus. Jesus worked at me for more than thirty years! He has been drawing me to Him since I was a little boy, when I knew nothing about God or religion because my family was nonobservant. Finally, in 2008, He gave me the last push, which enabled me to take the great plunge from the Torah into the Gospel. This is what I am going to describe in this book, the story of my life with God. Rereading it, I feel it is the story of a fool. "God chose what is foolish in the world" (1 Cor 1:27). Saint Paul says that. Does not God Himself often behave like a total fool in the Old and New Testaments—for example, when He asks His prophet Hosea to marry a prostitute? Saint Paul writes that what is folly in the eyes of men is wisdom in the eyes of God (see 1 Cor 1:18–30).

For as long as I can remember, I have been drawn to Jesus, so much so that as a teenager I wanted to convert to Christianity. But I knew that this would scandalize my family because when a Jew converts, his family, even if not religious, experiences it as a betrayal. God's ways are mysterious: I wanted to be a Christian, and I became an ultra-Orthodox Jew, and then a Hasidic Jew. My heart lead me to Jesus but my head refused to follow and my Jewish identity fought back hard. Finally at the end of a long development, one day God lifted a veil from my eyes. And then everything became clear—he gave me a "new" understanding, and I saw things in a different light.

9

This book tells the story of a conversion, but above all it is the story of a man who fought for a very long time against the Trinitarian God, who was waiting for him and giving him signs.

I was encouraged to write this account by many people to whom I spoke about my journey. At any rate, as the apostles Peter and John said to the priests who had arrested them and wanted to forbid them from pronouncing the Name of Jesus, it is impossible for me *not* to speak about what I have seen and heard. I am burning to share this discovery of Jesus, who has changed my life, and to share it widely, and not only with the people who attend the conferences I give on the Scriptures. The time has come to bear witness openly and without fear. I feel inwardly pushed to do so.

I address this testimony to all my brothers. First, to those who call themselves nonbelievers but who feel they are seeking God deep within without knowing who He is. I am thinking of some people who are reluctant to approach religion because it would cut them off from their families or their intellectual milieus. Some may be afraid of the Catholic Church, either because they see the Church in a bad light due to what the media reports about her, or because their Catholic parents passed on a narrow and false vision of the Gospel to them. Some may even imagine that the Church wants to confine them, to prevent them from being human, when it is just the *opposite*. I am also thinking of those who hold a grudge against Christians because of wrongs they have committed throughout history; I will return to this later.

I also address this book to my Jewish brothers, who, when they learned that I had converted, banned me from the Jewish community without trying to understand why I took this step and committed what is an unimaginable transgression for the ultra-Orthodox Hasidic Jew I was, who had been taught to hate Jesus. They thought that I was angry with the God of the Jews because of the ordeals I had gone through—not at all! Mine is not an exceptional case. Many Jews have converted, starting with the first apostles. I hope that my Jewish brothers, brothers according to the flesh, will have the curiosity or will do me the favor of reading what I have to say in order to try to understand. For it is so heartbreaking to hear it said or claimed that I have betrayed the faith of my people, when I love Judaism in all its parts and with every fiber of my being.

Finally, I wrote this book for my Christian brothers. I hope it will enliven their faith by bringing home to them how blessed they are to know this God who loves them as they are, this God who lets Himself be approached and loved, in a personal relationship, and not only through the observation of laws, important as they are. For that is truly the heart of Christianity and what Jesus revealed: the relationship of love between God and each one of us that changes our way of living with our brothers. I want to bear witness to this. I cannot keep silent about it.

I Did Not Even Know I Was Jewish

I was born June 10, 1964, at Lariboisière Hospital in Paris. My parents named me Jean-Marc: Jean, after my maternal grandfather, and Marc because my mother thought Jean by itself sounded a little old-fashioned. Without realizing it, my parents had given me the names of two evangelists (that is, John and Mark, respectively). I *definitely* see a veiled message from Providence in this. Moreover, was it an accident that, since I was sick, I was not circumcised on the eighth day as Jewish Law requires? I was circumcised when I was a year old. My grandfather Jean was my godfather. I do not know what Hebrew name I was given on that occasion, or even if I was given one.

It may be hard to believe, but for several years I was *totally* ignorant of being Jewish. And I was going to learn it in a rather unusual way. One day, at school, I began to call one of my classmates a "dirty Jew". The teacher punished me *very* severely. I found her reaction a little excessive; I did not understand why she was so upset. For me, it was an insult like any other. When I came home, I told my mother what happened. She looked at me and responded simply: "Jean-Marc, you are Jewish." End of story. What, me, I was Jewish? But what did that mean, "Jewish"?

In fact, I was living in what is called an assimilated Jewish family. My mother never celebrated Jewish feasts and fed us ham and pasta like any other French mother. At home, there was not a single Jewish book or object. Sure, my father carried on a few traditions, but he did not explain what they meant to us; thus for a long time, I did not realize that they were related to religion. That was how it was, for example, with the mezuzah attached to the lintel of our front door. I never really asked myself what it was all about. It was only much later, while becoming religiously observant, that I would learn that the mezuzah is a little parchment inscribed with verses from the Torah (Deut 6:4–9; 11:13–21) and inserted in a small case. Jews put it on the right side of their home's front door as a sign of protection. It recalls the last plague in Egypt, when Moses told the Hebrew people to put some lamb's blood on the lintel and the top of the door so that the exterminating angel who was to kill all the firstborn might spare their home.

Friday evenings, at the beginning of Shabbat (Jewish Sabbath), my father said a kiddush prayer, but a rather simplified one, to tell the truth. He put on the *kippah* (skullcap) and said a prayer lasting five or ten minutes, but I did not know what it meant. For us kids it was a solemn time, nothing more. We sensed only that it was *not* the time for being noisy. Later, much later, I would myself recite a kiddush, which is a prayer of sanctification for the Sabbath said by observant Jews when they come home on Friday evenings. When the father of the family comes back from synagogue, the mother welcomes him by lighting small candles. The whole family sings Shabbat songs, notably "Shalom Aleichem". Afterward a passage from chapter 31 of the Proverbs of King Solomon is read: "Who can find a good wife? She is far more precious than jewels. The heart of her husband trusts in her" (vv. 10–11). Then the father recites the kiddush, from *kadosh*, meaning "to be holy" or "to be set apart". This is how the Sabbath, which commemorates the day when God rested after having completed His Creation, is sanctified.

Next are prayers over the wine (and the grape juice for children), followed by the ablutions, when the hands are washed with water poured from a *keli* (a special vessel). Afterward is the blessing over the bread, which is challah, a kind of brioche prepared especially for Shabbat.* But, my family did not respect this whole ritual. Nor could it be said that my father really observed Shabbat since he sometimes went to Paris on Saturday using mass transit. He never went to synagogue. In fact, I assumed religion did not interest him.

When I was seven, my older brother began to prepare for his bar mitzvah. He took Talmud Torah classes, but at home he did not talk about it and my parents *never* asked him what he was learning. The day of the ceremony, we got up very early, at six in the morning, and put on our best outfits. I could tell that it was an important event. We went to synagogue, and my brother read the scrolls of the Torah in Hebrew. Afterward, we returned home, where my parents had organized a party. I did not really understand what it all meant. It was only two years later that I would really become aware of what I was, when I caught sight of my mother's anguished face before the television. She was watching the news. I could read fear in her gaze. Tanks were advancing in the desert; Arabs were entering Israel: it was the Yom Kippur War of 1973. I was nine, and for the *first* time I felt a sense of belonging to the Jewish people. This feeling was colored with anxiety, fear of seeing the State of Israel disappear.

---

* This bread commemorates the loaves "of the presence", the twelve loaves once offered in the name of the twelve tribes of Israel each Sabbath day by the priest and which he alone was authorized to eat the following Saturday. King David, when he was hungry one day, broke the prohibition, which Jesus recalls to the rabbis who were reproaching His disciples for gathering grains of wheat on the Sabbath (see Mk 2:23–28).

One day, when I was eleven, I asked my mother: "One of my classmates is hosting his German pen pal at home right now; can I invite them both over?" Immediately she answered very curtly: "No, he's a Jerry." What is a Jerry? I would have to wait until the following year to find out. It might seem strange, but until I entered seventh grade, I had never heard of extermination camps. My mother never told us what she lived through when she was little. However, without ever verbalizing it, she passed on a fear to us, the fear shared by the Jewish people, because of always having to fight for survival. What a mystery that this little people, after all the pogroms and persecutions it has suffered in Christian and Muslim countries, and even long before, should still exist, while the great empires that dominated the ancient world—Greece, Egypt, Rome— have come and gone.

Little by little while growing up, I discovered my family background. I was Ashkenazic through my mother, Sephardic through my father. My maternal grandfather emigrated from Romania and found refuge in France at the very beginning of the twentieth century. He fought so well in the French Army during the First World War that at his death in 1966 he was buried in the military cemetery at Bagneux. As for my maternal grandmother, she was of Polish origin. My mother was seven years old in 1939, when the Second World War began. Her family lived in Paris throughout the war. My grandfather was arrested on several occasions but miraculously released each time. When a roundup was being organized, the district police captain would warn him so that he could hide with his wife and six children (four girls and two boys). No one in their building ever denounced them either. I imagine it was because of what my mother lived through during those years that she, without being at all observant, so strongly asserted her Jewish identity, in contrast to my father.

I did not really know my maternal grandfather. He died when I was two. We regularly went to visit my grandmother at her home on Rue Alfonse Carr in Paris. She and my mother would have long discussions in Yiddish. For me, these were grown-up conversations. But I felt that if they were speaking in Yiddish, it was so that they would not be understood, and I was really curious what it was they wanted to hide from us. After the war, my maternal grandparents gave up the few traditions they had kept up when they arrived in France. So I did not receive a religious heritage from that side of the family. The only tradition that my mother kept from her parents was culinary: she would prepare stuffed cabbage for us.

My father was born in Tunisia in 1929. At the end of the forties, around the age of eighteen, he came to spend a vacation in France and stayed there. His parents joined him afterward. We frequently went to my paternal grandparents' place for lunch; they lived by the Ledru-Rollin metro stop. My grandfather was very welcoming. He always had a big smile on his face when he opened the door. He often played the French card game Belote with us. My grandmother, on the other hand, was more reserved, but she cooked us good Mediterranean dishes: chickpea bouillon in the winter, turnip and carrot salads, and of course, the couscous that my mother learned to cook from her. I loved my grandparents very much, but I did not know much about them. They never talked about Tunisia. And then, the idea of asking my father questions about his youth never occurred to me: we did not talk much about ourselves in my family. My grandparents ate kosher, but that was something I would know only much later. Passing on the Jewish traditions that they maintained did not seem to be a priority for them either.

A Jewish Kid from the Projects

During the first years of my life I lived with my parents, my big brother, and my big sister in a little two-room flat on Rue du Faubourg Poissonnière in Paris. A narrow staircase led up to our apartment. The toilet and shower, which we shared with the neighbors, were on the landing. Then, little by little, my mother succeeded in convincing my father to move. It was not easy but she was persistent. She was the one who took care of all that needed to be done at home and who took the initiative for the family. So she went to city hall to seek other housing.

That was how, a little later, after the birth of my baby brother, she brought me on a preview visit to our new apartment. It was located in La Courneuve in a brand-new block of the Cité des 4,000.* Upon arriving at the housing project, I was mesmerized by the sensation of looming space. It really seemed so enormous, compared to the old Parisian neighborhood where we had lived until then. It was also very clean. This La Courneuve housing project was part of the low-income housing of the city of Paris; that was why it was kept up so well. We were not even allowed to walk on the grass. When I discovered our new apartment, I was amazed: it was huge and bright. In my eyes it was a real palace. Make note of one last detail that was going be a determining factor in my life: from my bedroom window I could see Sacré-Cœur Basilica in Montmartre.

* The Cité des 4,000 is a four-thousand-person housing project in La Courneuve (a commune in northern Paris).

It was here that my little sister would be born. Fifteen years later, this housing block where I grew up would be the first destroyed in order to make way for smaller buildings, which would be a great media event. I was happy in this housing project, where I would spend my childhood and adolescence. Of course, the population changed through the years. But I never felt any form of racism or anti-Semitism, or rivalries between communities. We organized soccer games where Jewish and Muslim teams competed, but this all went on in a spirit of true camaraderie. Occasionally we mixed communities and formed teams by building.

At Courneuve, moreover, everybody knew we were Jewish; my mother did not hide it from our neighbors. Even so we did not forge ties with the other Jewish families in the housing project. On the other hand, we had Muslim friends. One evening my brother got a fishbone caught in his throat. Everybody panicked. We rushed over to ring the doorbell of our neighbor down the hall, a Jewish doctor, to ask for his help. He came immediately and saved my brother's life. But despite this episode, we did not develop a close relationship with him.

It was my mother who took care of us and made the decisions affecting us. She also looked after other children at our home in order to make a little money. She was not an especially affectionate mother, but she put me at ease. She held down the fort, as they say. She was a devoted wife who never complained. Saturday she would go to do the shopping at the Aubervilliers market that was a mile from our place. Sometimes I went along with her to help with the bags. She was the one who organized our vacations, visited the travel agencies, supervised our schooling, and filled out administrative forms. My father, for his part, left early in the morning and came home late at night. He was a leather craftsman and worked for the big leather business Pourchet on Rue du Faubourg du Temple. He did not communicate with us much. One day he brought me to the movie theater with my brother to see *Gunfight at the O.K. Corral*, with Burt Lancaster and Kirk Douglas, but that was an exception.

An Unusual Child

I was a very introverted little boy. I had never heard God talked about and yet I would talk to Him. I would say to Him: "My God, my God." He was the one who was there, and to whom I could talk inside myself. I liked being alone. On vacation, I preferred walking alone, looking at the sea, the horizon, out where there was nothing but silence. The infinite attracted me, and first of all through landscapes. At night, I would gaze at the moon for a long time in silence, and I would contemplate what was behind it. God, in the beginning, I looked for in the sky. My mother would gently poke fun at me: "What are you looking for in the sky? Jean-Marc, you've got your head in the clouds!" She said this attraction to the sky corresponded to my zodiac sign, the Gemini, who fly. Often, in the evening, I would look out of my bedroom window toward the Sacré-Cœur Basilica. I dreamed about living in a little mountain village, with its church and its parish priest, as in the *Heidi* book I loved. To me it was an ideal place, which was strange because it is *not* at all the image that Jews have of an earthly paradise.

I had a friendly face and long hair, like many children in the seventies. I was cheerful; I laughed a lot. I lived in my own little world, which made me a little different from my peers but did not prevent me from having friends. My best friend, Y., who was in my class, lived on the fifteenth floor of our building. He was Muslim. We had a very strong friendship. His family knew I was Jewish, but they always made me feel very welcome in their home. His mother was observant and wore the headscarf. She prayed five times a day and observed Ramadan. But Y. and I did not talk about religion when we were together. We sensed that we were different, and we did not want to have a falling out. During the Yom Kippur War, we did not talk about Israel.

The two of us would have a lot of fun. Y. was very good at judo, and I was on the handball team. And we played soccer, of course; we talked soccer. In the evenings, the two of us would practice in the housing project, with a bottle of Coke in hand.

In many respects, I was like any other kid. I liked Westerns, detective films, and the songs that came on the radio. I collected stamps. But the only thing I was really passionate about besides God was soccer. I was "in deep", as they say. I would play it outside and watch games on television, sometimes alone. I knew all the teams by heart. I loved the players Jean-Michel Larqué, Dominique Rocheteau, and Ivan Curkovic. I watched the World Cup and the European Cup. In August, when we were on vacation in Vendée, I waited impatiently for the Wednesday night championship games. I remember watching Saint-Étienne play against Kiev and the Saint-Étienne/Bavaria game, 0–1; I can see all over again the free kick they made in the first half. And the Saint-Étienne and Liverpool game—Liverpool had the ball; Keegan lobbed it over Curkovic, Saint-Étienne's goalkeeper, in the second half. Saint-Étienne scored with a kick from the halfway line by Bathenay that lobbed over Klemens, Liverpool's goalkeeper. Saint-Étienne lost, but Bathenay's score, from the halfway line, with the left foot, was fantastic!

At school I was less joyful, and that drove my mother absolutely crazy. I enjoyed recess and had lots of friends, but my grades were bad. I did not like the way the school was organized, the very methodical way of proceeding, and the fact that you had to work to get good grades. All that did not seem essential to me, really. In fact, I only studied what interested me: I read the math and physics books. In French, on the other hand, I was terrible.

One day the teacher called in my mother and told her: "Jean-Marc is ridiculing me. He's smart but he pretends not to understand. Today he got a bad grade on his math test. I had him go up to the chalkboard for the corrections, and then he gave me all the answers without hesitating!" I saw clearly that my mother was beside herself. What had been going on in my head? I think I did not really see the reason for taking a test—I had been looking out the window.

It was suspected that I was dyslexic. So my mother brought me to a speech pathologist. I played some games there. It was a lot of fun, but I am not sure it helped much. My mother was worried about me and kept a closer eye on me than she did the others. As a result my brothers and sisters thought I was her favorite.

Christmas Lights

What I loved more than anything else at school was the Christmas party. The snow, the tree in the classroom—to me it was a wonderful atmosphere. I really wanted to have a Christmas tree at home. Even as an adult, Christmas would always be my favorite holiday. Does not Jesus say to become a child again, a child of God, in order to enter His kingdom? This is what the Christmas holiday expresses. God works through the senses. Thus my sensitivity at Christmas is connected with the importance of the Incarnation. God became man, in flesh and blood, with a human heart that cried, suffered, loved, and rejoiced. Did I realize that Christmas is a Christian holiday? Yes, of course. At school they explained to us that Christmas commemorates the birth of Jesus. That was how I knew somewhat about Jesus.

Strangely, my mother, who as I said did not celebrate a single Jewish holiday, would gather her brothers and sisters on Christmas Eve. That was her own way of being French. She would get up during the night to put our gifts in the living room. On the other hand, there was no question of putting up a tree in the house. It would have been unthinkable: for her, the tree was a Christian symbol. The Christmas Eve family gatherings were always full of warmth. My mother's two brothers would be there with their children, my cousins, whom we actually saw regularly. They would bring gifts for me. I had a special attachment to one of my aunts, the wife of one of my mother's brothers. I sensed that she really liked me, though I could not say why. She would always maintain her affection for me; later, she supported me when I wanted to leave for Israel against my parents' advice. My mother also had a sister, Marie, but she was never invited. She lived in the United States. I found out, by overhearing conversations, that she had become Catholic and that my mother had disowned her. But the topic was taboo. All of this left me confused: Why did we celebrate this Christian holiday when we were not allowed to say my aunt's name because she had become Catholic?

One Christmas Eve, my mother sent me to buy bread at the bakery. I saw this as a great pretext for making a short detour in the direction of the church. I went there calmly, trying to keep my indifferent expression so that no one would ask me what I was up to. When I arrived in front of the door, I glanced discreetly inside. My heart began to beat faster—I so wanted to go in!

My Best Friend Jesus

I had my first encounter with Jesus while on summer vacation in Brittany; I was eight years old. There was a cross affixed to the wall in my bedroom; and inexplicably, I felt drawn to Christ. Yet I did not even know much about Him. Of course I recognized the cross from having seen it on bell towers at churches, the places where Christians met, but I did not understand its significance. I became completely obsessed with this cross, which drew me to it like a magnet. During the day, I would go back to my room frequently and remain there contemplating it. Obviously, I would go when I was alone so that the others would not discover what I was doing. I was well aware that my family was not Christian, and I had the vague impression of doing something I was not supposed to do. But the attraction was stronger than I was; I felt so good before the cross that I could have stayed there for hours.

The following summer we went on vacation to Sables-d'Olonne. On the roads in Vendée, I noticed enormous, very imposing Calvary scenes at every crossroads. I was captivated. So while the others were napping after lunch, I would secretly go out for a walk to meet the man on the cross. As soon as I arrived at one of the roadside Calvary scenes, I would stop and plant myself there. Gazing at Christ, I was completely under His spell. I would admire Him, contemplate Him, and love Him. Sometimes I talked to Him, but not always. Afterward, when I went back to the house where we were staying, I would lie upon the broad wall that bordered the patio and, with my arms stretched out as on a cross, think of Jesus.

Already at that time I felt that Jesus was calling me. And for my part, I was looking for Him. When I was home at La Courneuve, at night, I would wait for everyone to fall asleep and then, in the stillness that I loved so much, at the foot of my bed, I would slowly make my own sign of the cross. I loved making the sign of the cross. All day long, I would wait for this appointment. It was as if I were in love with Christ on the cross, this cross that would nevertheless become a scandal in my eyes when I was an Orthodox Jew. As a little boy I did not define this attraction that came from the depths of my heart or my soul. I was not in contact with any Christian who could have explained to me what the cross represented. But I was not yet asking myself questions. I was content to live this experience. I could spend hours looking at a crucifix. What I experienced in the presence of Jesus on the cross was extraordinary. At no time did I associate the cross with suffering or blood (even if, objectively, Jesus was in a state of torment). I did not even understand what it represented; what I felt was of a different order. I had the strong impression of being in contact with a person. It was a divine presence, a very powerful presence who pardoned, reconciled, gave peace, and brought me a deep interior sense of well-being. It was as if I were before the gates of Heaven. But all of this remained secret, in my child's heart.

I would keep this secret for thirty years. With hindsight, I ask myself: "Why, Lord, did I fall in love with an object of repugnance for my people, why?" This question would bore into me for a long time. "Grace makes use of every kind of kindling!" they say. One day when I was telling a friend about my life, she quoted this retort of French film director Michel Audiard: "Blessed are the cracked, for they let the light shine through." It does not bother me if this is what some people think. Saint Paul, for his part, said: "God chose what is foolish in the world to shame the wise, God chose what is weak in the world to shame the strong" (1 Cor 1:27). It is wonderful that we can never explain everything: there will always be this mystery between us and God, for God is unfathomable and all that human understanding can say about Him is but a drop of water in comparison to His enormity. Recalling these moments with Christ from my childhood, I understand better what Jesus said: "[U]nless you turn and become like children, you will never enter the kingdom of heaven" (Mt 18:3). The child is whole, without dissemblance; he trusts his inner voice. Pride, anger, rationalization—these have not yet smothered the still small voice.

Little by little I began to dream about going inside a church. In fifth grade I went on a class ski trip to Méaudre, near Grenoble in the Alps, for ten days. I felt so good in that mountain village with its church. On Sunday, the teacher asked who wanted to go to Mass, and although I burned with desire to go along, I did not dare to raise my hand.

A little while later, my family and I went to Estepona, Spain, to visit my father's brother who lived there. He was married to a Catholic. It was at that time, at the age of eleven, that I first entered a church, with my cousin. I was amazed: it was full of gorgeous crucifixes. I had a great desire to sit down in order to admire everything down to the least details, but I held back: I did not want to reveal my interest. We stayed only five minutes.

It is touching to think back on all of this. My desire was so strong, pure, and obvious. It was nothing but love.

Escapade at Sacré-Cœur in Montmartre

Like every Jewish boy, I began preparing for my bar mitzvah at the age of twelve. This is the ceremony by which a boy becomes an adult on the religious level. After his bar mitzvah, a Jewish man is responsible for fulfilling the commandments of the Torah. I was thus going to Talmud Torah classes every Sunday and Wednesday, with my Hebrew book and a notebook. Every class lasted four hours, but unlike school, I did not find it a burden at all. In these classes I learned to decode the Hebrew alphabet and then to read texts from the Bible. We had teachings on Genesis and the patriarchs (Abraham, Isaac, Jacob), and on the Exodus and Moses, as well as on Jewish history (Joshua, David, the Babylonian Captivity, and so forth). We also had to become familiar with the meaning of Jewish feasts, prayers, and the Law.

I was enormously interested in these classes. I liked to study the Bible. At that time in my life Judaism fulfilled me; I did not need anything else. If you reread the story of the conversion of Saint Paul, you can clearly see that he was a totally fulfilled Jew and a happy Pharisee. It was the same for me. These classes made me ask many questions about my family: Why did my mother not eat kosher? Why did we not follow Jewish traditions? And since we were after all such nonobservant Jews, why were we not allowed to say Jesus' name at home?

Despite these questions, this discovery of Judaism in no way interfered with my attraction to Christ. Deep within me, I still had the desire to push open the door of a church and find myself inside. Like Alice passing through the looking glass, I dreamed of entering that other dimension. Little by little, I decided to act on my desires. It was no small thing: I was aware of the risk I was running if I were ever caught in the act. In fact, I knew that if my parents discovered that I was attracted to Jesus, they would fly into a terrible rage. They would not have been willing to listen to me or to try to understand me; they would have seen none of the intensity and the beauty of what I was experiencing. Just the opposite: they would have done everything in their power to distance me from this source of life offering itself to me. My secret would have been revealed and ridiculed. It would have been a catastrophe.

Even so, I was ready to take the risk; I began making a plan. There was no question of going into the church near my home. Someone might see me and tell my parents about it. So I decided to go to Sacré-Cœur on a Sunday afternoon. It was far enough away from my home and big enough that I could blend in with the crowd without being noticed.

So it was that one sunny Sunday I put my plan into action. I took the train from La Courneuve to the Gare du Nord. Everything was buzzing around in my head. The thought of running into someone I knew who would ask where I was going was making me very nervous. And at the same time, I finally felt that I existed. I was happier than ever and aware of being in the middle of committing an important act. I got out at the Barbès metro stop and asked a passerby the direction to Sacré-Cœur. There it was; I was there. I went up the steps slowly, filled with emotion. I had waited so long for this moment that I wanted to savor it. So I took my time, looking about. I was relieved because there were a lot of people. I followed the crowd, like a tourist.

When I entered the basilica, the first thing that I noticed was the overwhelming darkness. Compared to the inside of synagogues, it seemed dark to me. So much the better— that way I would not run the risk of being recognized. I felt good; my fear had disappeared. I was not thinking especially about God. I was like a little kid amazed and overjoyed at finding Christmas lights. I looked every- where, my eyes seeking out a crucifix. Suddenly, I had a funny feeling. I felt so good in the church, as if I were at home. Yet it was at the synagogue that I was supposed to feel good. No matter! I did not want the moment to stop. I walked all around the basilica several times. Something like the scent of perfume was floating in the air. I liked the scent. I was happy. I was at home, finally at home.

On the left side, to the right at the end of the aisle, I noticed a Madonna and Child. I felt drawn to it. I did not know exactly who she was, but I knew that she was somehow tied to Jesus. Then I went to sit down and looked up at Him in the cupola—Him, on the cross. I stopped thinking of anything else; I wanted only to remain in His presence. I did not know Him but He knew me. I did not want to leave. At last, I had to force myself to leave Sacré- Cœur; it was like being torn away. I asked God, "Why all this heartbreak?" But at the same time I was filled with a deep interior joy. As the Psalm says: "One thing have I asked of the LORD, that will I seek after; that I may dwell in the house of the LORD" (27:4). Before leaving, I made a visit to the gift shop. I looked at the magazines and espe- cially the crucifixes. I really wanted to buy one to wear around my neck, but I had no money.

As I was going home, I decided to go back to Sacré- Cœur regularly. So, all week long at school, I looked

forward to my Sunday appointment. Waiting for that
moment, I got up each night when everyone was asleep
and knelt at the foot of my bed. I made the sign of the
cross, visualized Christ, and told Him that I loved Him.
There was absolutely no doubt that this was the best part
of my day. More and more, I felt the need to share all of
this with someone. So I decided to write to a particular girl
in my class who I knew was Catholic. Her mother ran the
bookstore next to the church where I would go to buy the
papers for my father. I scrawled "I love Christ, Jesus. Can
you help me?" on a piece of paper and dropped it in her
mailbox. When she still had not written back a few days
later, I went to see her in the schoolyard:

"Did you get my note?"

"Yes."

"Why didn't you write back?"

"Because I don't know how I can help you. . . ."

From that point on, I returned to Sacré-Cœur once a
month. I would walk around, sit, and stare to my heart's
content. Each time, I was filled with the same feeling
of well-being. One day I approached a nun, intending
to talk to her. But at the last moment, I lost my nerve
and abandoned the idea. Another time, I did the Way of
the Cross on my knees. At each station, I looked up at the
images, rapt.

My First Communion

It was December and I would be thirteen soon. My bar mitzvah was a few months away. It was a Sunday and once again I arrived at Sacré-Cœur Basilica. As usual, I sat down in one of the first rows. Suddenly the organ began to play. I did not dare move. I heard something like little bells: Mass was beginning! I was not sure what was going to happen but I stayed there. I heard readings that were familiar to me: verses from the Old Testament followed by a psalm. At one point the people around me—men, women, and children of all ages—stood and approached the altar, falling on their knees along the railing that separated them from the priest. Then they received something in their mouths from his hands. I had *no* idea what it was.

And then, I felt literally pushed from inside to stand up, to join the line, and to receive for myself this food about whose nature and meaning I was totally ignorant. All the same I was a little nervous because I was not sure what to do. I was afraid the priest would find me out me if I did not do the right thing. I noticed that the people murmured something before receiving the divine Host in their mouths, but I could not hear what it was they were saying. So I placed myself at the end of the row, on the right, and listened carefully. When I realized that they were responding "Amen", I felt very relieved. "Oh, it's not complicated; it's one of our words!" I said to myself.

Incredible as it may seem, this was how I received the Body of Christ for the first time, without knowing it and

within a few months before committing myself to obedience
to the God of the Torah. Ignorant of the contradiction,
my actions did not trouble my conscience at all. Rather,
after having received the Host, I was filled with a great
joy. I left the basilica truly happy. I already felt the desire
to go back for more. From that moment on, the Eucharist
became something like a drug for me. Here is another
of God's follies. He allowed me to receive Communion
and to experience some of its effects—closeness to God,
peace, and joy—even though the Church does not permit
reception of the Eucharist until after baptism.

Months went by, during which I received Communion
regularly, and in June, as planned, I had my bar mitzvah.
Actually, since my father did not have enough money to
pay a rabbi to come to the synagogue, to read the Torah,
and to lead a big party, as had happened for my brother's
bar mitzvah, he took me to a synagogue in Paris where
he knew the rabbi, and we did the bare minimum. I put
on the large shawl that Jewish men put on every day for
morning prayer, said the blessing on the phylacteries and
on the shawl, and recited the Shema Israel: "Hear, O Israel:
the Eternal One is our God, the Eternal One is one alone"
(see Deut 6:4). That was it. I did not say anything to my
father, but I was extremely irritated to have a cut-rate bar
mitzvah. Fortunately my parents still invited family over,
and I received a few gifts: my uncle, my mother's brother,
gave me a desk (which would later become my daughter
Déborah's), and my father gave me a watch. I also received
a camera and some money. Yet I was still disappointed by
the way the great ceremony had gone.

In total I received 150 francs (approximately 30 U.S.
dollars). I immediately thought of the gift shop at Sacré-
Cœur. At *last* I could buy myself a cross. I was scared to
think what would happen if my father, mother, brothers,

or sisters discovered it, and yet I was determined. I did not know where this strength came from. Was I being irresponsible? Maybe, but so what? So I went to buy a big 1.5-inch gold cross. I would wear it around my neck secretly under my shirt and touch it all day long. I could not get over it myself. It was unbelievable; I was wearing a cross! At night I would hide it under my pillow. Having Jesus with me at all times made me very happy. But at the same time, I was constantly afraid of being found out. Waking up in the morning, I would be afraid that my cross had fallen on the floor, or I would be afraid of forgetting it under my pillow, where my mother might find it while making the bed.

And what had to happen, happened. During summer vacation, in Vendée, I woke up one morning and realized that my cross was missing. Panicked, I looked for it everywhere: under my bed, under the mattress. It was hopeless; I could not find it. I was dead meat! A few minutes later, my brother found it and brought it to my mother. My heart was racing. I could tell that a big scene was going to erupt. I listened to the conversation from a distance:

"Mom, I found this under Jean-Marc's bed!"

"Show me. It must belong to the people who rented before us."

Phew, I was burning up! There was a kind of false bottom in the drawer of the desk my uncle had given me. I hid in it some postcards showing a church topped with a cross. Later, when I was going to Israel, I took them along so that they would not be found, and I threw them away there.

When I went to Mass at Sacré-Cœur I would hear the Gospel read. I quickly realized that it was a book that talked about the life of Jesus. Eager to know Christ better, I decided to buy myself a New Testament. I chose a paperback version with a soft cover with a picture of blue and orange mountains. I was so happy to have one of my own. I felt like I was holding a treasure. Whenever I had the chance—for the most part, in the metro on the way to school—I dove eagerly into the texts, as I would have read a storybook. Saint John's Gospel was my favorite. I began to learn it by heart. I had a contemplative way of reading: as I read, I would connect myself to the Person of Jesus. But for the time being I did not ask myself about putting His Word into practice.

Starting with the seventh grade, I was sent to school at a Jewish institution far from our home. It was in this school that, at the same time I was discovering Jesus, I got to know Judaism better and became passionate about that world. It was there, too, that I began to pray and to practice the Jewish Law.

Jewish or Christian?

My mother enrolled me in the private Jewish school because my parents were afraid that I was becoming a hoodlum. They made the decision the day the police came and rang our doorbell. With a gang of friends, I had thrown some stones and broken the windowpanes of a house. That was the final straw. My father gave me a good dressing-down.

I was happy in this new middle school and worked harder than before. In fact, my attraction to Christianity paradoxically encouraged my interest in the religion of my forefathers. I studied Jewish history, the Bible, and Hebrew. A whole world was opening up before me. For the first time, I heard about the Shoah (Holocaust), which aroused a strong nationalism in me. I started feeling a great love for Israel. I found an identity for myself, a sense of belonging to the Jewish people—my people. I learned that France largely collaborated in rounding up the Jews. Why then had my mother remained in France? From that time on, because of the persecution-marked history of the Jews, I began to perceive non-Jews as potential enemies. That was how I wound up adhering to religious Zionism.

It is hard to understand this, but the divine presence that I felt at Sacré-Cœur had nothing to do with the God I was coming to know at school. At school, I invoked God with Jewish prayers. In the evenings, alone in my room, when I knelt at the foot of my bed and made the sign of the cross, it was much more than a simple prayer:

it was a relationship, a meeting with someone. Friday and Saturday mornings, I went to synagogue; Sunday, to Sacré-Cœur. At first it did not seem like a conflict to me, but sure enough, little by little this double life became unbearable. I felt that Christ and the Torah were contradictory. So, at the age of fifteen, I decided to come out with everything, to provoke a scandal.

So it was that after a mature reflection I went to Sacré-Cœur resolved to open my heart to a priest. I felt very anxious and worried. But I was not going to turn back; I was not going to take a step backward. As I came into the basilica I was afraid; my heart was beating so fast I thought it would break. I was aware of having made an important, irreversible decision. But, it was bigger than I was: I wanted to convert and to become a priest. I took stock of the magnitude of the scandal that this choice would provoke and I took it upon myself. I had but one desire: to be Christian! I sat down in the nave, looking at Jesus and speaking to Him. Then I gathered up all my courage and very quickly, so as not to change my mind, rose and went and knelt in a confessional. I made the sign of the cross and waited. I could hear my heart thumping in my chest. Finally the priest spoke to me:

"I am listening, my son."

"I'm Jewish and I want to be Christian."

"Wh—What?!"

I repeated with greater strength and confidence: "I am Jewish and I wish to convert." There it was; I had said it. For a few seconds, I felt so happy! I was filled with great peace. But this beatific state did not last. It would appear that the Lord had decided that the moment for my conversion had not yet come. As it happened, the priest left the confessional like a Jack-in-the-box. He looked at me with a panicked expression and told me: "Don't move; wait for me. I'm coming back!"

He went away toward the right side, in the direction of the sacristy, leaving me stuck there, alone. It was horrible. A feeling of distress came over me. Why had he not understood that I was expecting him to take me by the hand and to bring me with him to the sacristy? Had he not realized the superhuman effort I had just made in order to talk to him? The wait seemed endless to me, and my thoughts started running. My reason was winning out; it told me that I was making an enormous mistake and that I could not betray my Jewish identity. Suddenly, I could not stand it anymore: I rose and went away, upset. Did the priest come back? I will never know.

I was distraught. But despite everything, I continued to show up at Sacré-Cœur every Sunday. I regularly attended Mass and received the Body of Christ. During those times, my thoughts would stop completely; I felt good. Inside, I still had a strong desire to convert, but I told myself that any conversion would have to happen very fast without my having the time to reflect. This double life would last until I was eighteen.

Jewish and Christian

Little by little between the ages of fifteen and eighteen I became an observant Jew. By applying the Jewish Law I introduced God, who had always been at the heart of my thoughts, to my daily life. From that point on, I lived in a world divided into two parts: on one side there were the pagans and on the other the Jews. Progressively, this led me to cut myself off from the world. Since I was eating kosher, for example, I could no longer eat with non-Jews. Likewise, I decided to give up handball because the games took place on Saturday.

At home these changes made for an electric atmosphere. I wore the kippah and ate my meals separately. I had my own kosher dishware. I would prepare my Shabbat meal on my own based on deli meats and french fries, and on Saturdays when my mother turned on the television I would leave the room and go to my bedroom. Tuesdays and Fridays, I went to synagogue alone. My parents did not look kindly on any of this. One day my father began to tap his finger on the table, exclaiming: "We're not going to have a rabbi in the home!" My mother, too, was firmly opposed to my becoming religious. It was hard on them. Indeed by observing the Law that they were not applying, I was implicitly showing them how they ought to behave. In some ways this inverted the normal relationship between parents and children, in which the parents teach their children what to do. I also argued a lot with my older sister. That was because she was going out with a *goy*, a non-Jew. So I would preach at her. Sometimes we spoke about politics. She was far Left, did theater, and was becoming ideologically close to pro-Palestinian movements. That drove me crazy. I could not accept her going against the Jewish people. You can imagine what it was like!

Little by little I also distanced myself from my friends, including my best friend, Y. The summer that I was fifteen, when I was not yet wearing the kippah or eating kosher, we went on vacation to Algeria together. The two of us took the train to Marseilles, then the boat. His big sister who lived in Algiers hosted us. Then, shortly after, one Friday evening when we were watching television at his place, we happened upon a program talking about Islam. A Frenchman was explaining why he had become Muslim. This testimony struck me deeply—so deeply that I read the Koran from A to Z, long before reading the Bible, which I knew only in fragments. The following summer, we went away together again to Ibiza, with our big brothers. But despite everything, we progressively grew apart. I began wearing the kippah. I stopped going out on Fridays or Saturdays because I was keeping Shabbat and stopped dining at his place because I was eating kosher. The Jewish Law cut me off from him. But he also found it hard to accept that I had become a religious Jew. I understood this; it was natural: we tend to associate with people who share our own values. For my part, I made new friends who had the same interests as I at the Jewish school. Nevertheless, thinking back over it, I tell myself we should learn how to love each person as he is and not as we wish he were. This is in any case what Jesus asks of us. He teaches us to love everyone, even those who do not share our views. He even asks us to go further and to love our enemies. Saint Paul wrote: "Bless those who persecute you" (Rom 12:14).

Everywhere I went I felt like a hair in a bowl of soup. I lived in an interior monastery in the midst of others. It was not that I did not like relating to people anymore but that I thought of myself as no longer sharing the same areas of interest as others. My old friends would reproach me and exclaim: "We can't talk soccer with you anymore!" Yes, I still liked soccer, but it was no longer my number one passion. What interested me was the Bible, Israel, and my relationship with God. I had not chosen it myself; it happened on its own. All I did was say yes to this passion for Jesus. My dream was to be with Christ. It was just like being in love, when you think only of the person you are in love with and forget friends and family. And if the family is opposed to this love and you have to make a choice, you choose the girl you love. The only thing I told Jesus was that I loved Him. It was an exclusive relationship from one beloved to another—as in the Song of Songs. As a result I was not at all tempted to go out to nightclubs and flirt with girls, as would my friends and my brother. Girls would come later.

Was I perhaps a precocious mystic? I have no idea. I was discovering that God loved me and that I loved Him. For the time being, I was in a two-way relationship. Later, I would understand that God also loves me through other people and that He asks me to love Him by loving others. When God addressed Saul, He said to him: "[W]hy do *you* persecute me?" (Acts 9:4, emphasis added). Yet Saul was not persecuting God *directly*; he was persecuting the Christians. But when you persecute a child of God, it is God you hurt. God is such that He has chosen to be loved by our loving others: "[A]s you did it to one of the least of these my brethren, you did it to me" (Mt 25:40), he says. But at that time, I was not there yet.

On one side there was Jesus; on the other, Israel. At school, I participated in a Bible contest. The first prize was a trip to Israel. I was so motivated that I won. I carried off the contest on biblical texts by a *large* margin. However, my parents refused to let me go to Israel. My mother used the pretext that there was a war and that it was too dangerous. I could not understand her preventing me from achieving this dream. I was unhappy.

At eighteen my schooling was finished. I had given it plenty of thought: if I was so drawn to God, it was better to seek Him in my own religion. I did not wish to pursue rabbinical formation in France. I wanted to go to the source itself, to the Holy Land. So I decided to leave for Israel. At first, my mother did not at all approve of my decision. Against all expectations, however, she wound up accepting that I was going; maybe she understood the Zionist call? Or maybe she was in some way relieved that I was leaving the home where my religious engagement caused so many difficulties. For whatever reason, she was the one who purchased the airplane ticket and covered the travel costs of my first year there.

That was how I sacrificed the love of Christ for Israel. I would stay there for eight years. At the end of the first year, I requested Israeli citizenship. I rejected France. Israel was our country, for us, the Jews. I was in full search of my identity. I certainly did not understand why my mother had remained in France after World War II. For me, the French were Nazi collaborators. It was only later that I would learn that French men and women of all stripes, including Christians and priests, had saved Jews.

An Israeli Rabbi

It was 1982; I was eighteen and on a plane for Israel. I was going there under the auspices of Bnei Akiva, a Zionist program spread out over three years: the first year on a kibbutz (a communal farm), the second in a yeshiva (a school for the study of the Torah and the Talmud), and the third in the army. We were a whole group of friends from my school who joined up with young Jewish men and women from Marseille, Lyon, and Belgium. Upon arriving, we first spent a month learning Hebrew and Jewish culture at an *ulpan* (the Hebrew word for "instruction") in a village named Hadera, in Haifa District. The ulpan program was set up by the Education Ministry when the State of Israel was formed, in order to serve new immigrants and even Jewish tourists. We learned rudimentary Hebrew and said our prayers. We were shown all around Israel in order to see the country. During this first month, I made new friends who came from all kinds of countries, and I flirted with an English Jew. And yes, even in Israel, English girls are popular.

Afterward, we left for the kibbutz. Ours was in the middle of the countryside not far from the Jordanian border. Nor was it far from the Jordan River, where Jesus was baptized, but of course I did not know that yet. In the distance you could see the mountains of Moab described in the Bible. We were about thirty young people, fifteen boys and fourteen girls, and we lived together like one big family. Our lifestyle was fairly Spartan, but the atmosphere was free, joyful, and warm. Two counselors, a man and a woman, supervised us, leading our activities and training. The mornings were devoted to the study of Hebrew, Jewish philosophy, the Bible, and the Talmud. We had prayers. Sometimes, we went on outings. The rest of the time I worked the earth, and there in the fields my solitary and contemplative side was reawakened. We had to install big irrigation pipes across carrot seedbeds. I liked the outdoor work because it allowed me to contemplate God in these incredible surroundings. I would often stop in the middle of work on the tractor and breathe deeply while looking around. I was as happy as a child. Now and again the others would call out to me: "Élie, Élie, what are you up to?" Yes, Élie, because I had chosen a Jewish first name when I arrived in Israel. I had had enough of Jean-Marc.

In the evenings, our training continued. We were required to read the Israeli news or watch it on television, even if we did not understand any of it at first. The intent of course was to familiarize us with the language, and I did learn Hebrew very quickly. After the news we would debate religious or political questions. We were not always in agreement. For example, some of us thought that it would be necessary to cede territories and others did not. Among us there were young people from the Left and the Right, a happy mix. As for me, I saw myself aligned with the right-wing, religious Zionist party, Mafdal.

At the heart of the kibbutz, we each had an adopted family we could go to if we needed anything. The wife of my host couple was of French origin; the husband had come from Romania. Sometimes I would have coffee with them or share their meal in the cafeteria. For the very festive feast of Purim, which commemorates the miraculous salvation of the Jews when they were ruled by Persia, an episode told in the Book of Esther (see 9:26–32),

I dressed up and drank with the husband. But I spent most of my time with my friends. I forged brotherly ties of friendship with them. During work and study, boys and girls were mixed. Even though we were sleeping in separate buildings, at night we would have water fights with the girls or smear their rooms with toothpaste. The atmosphere was that of a college fraternity. We had big, open spaces and free time at our disposal. I had a girlfriend, D., whom I wanted to marry. We shared the same political views and enjoyed each other's company.

And Christ, was I thinking about Him? Since I was surrounded by Jews, not really. But, like a passionate love that you have decided to forget and reawakens when something reminds you of it, I thought about Jesus again when we went on pilgrimage to Jerusalem. My attraction to Him was intact. It was as if I were magnetized but trying to resist. It was a strange feeling. During that year on the kibbutz, we walked around a lot in the north of Israel, and each time, I wanted to go into the Arab towns in Galilee because I knew that I would find Christians there.

I was so happy at the kibbutz that I even imagined spending the rest of my life there. I liked the communal life that frees you from every material concern. However, my intent was to learn a lot and then to teach. That was why I was going to a leave for a yeshiva, while some of my friends were going to participate in community service in developing cities.

At Torah School

So it was that at the end of a year, I packed my bags again, this time to settle in the suburbs of Hebron in the West Bank, where the religious Zionist yeshiva of Kiryat Arba is located.

On one of my very first days, I decided to go out alone from the *yishuv*, the Jewish settlement, to visit the tomb of the patriarchs Abraham, Isaac, and Jacob in the city of Hebron. I enjoyed my outing. Upon my return, to my great surprise, I was strongly reprimanded. It was made known to me that I had taken a great risk in going out alone while wearing my kippah into the city of Hebron, which was teeming with Arabs. I had gone there in complete ignorance, not at all aware of the danger. From that point on, whenever we went to Hebron, we were always accompanied by armed men. I saw Muslims in the streets but had no contact with them. For me, the Palestinians were just a concept. During that first year at the yeshiva, I heard airplanes flying above us and talk about the war in Lebanon, but I was not really interested in it. Studying the Torah took all I had. Even so, I had not broken up with my girlfriend D.; we were still together, as they say. We saw each other when possible, and we called each other on the telephone.

The atmosphere at the yeshiva was not at all like that on the kibbutz. In effect, all interaction with the other students, the young and not so young, came through Torah study. Nevertheless it was a very warm atmosphere. The

47

person in charge of the yeshiva was of American origin and very welcoming. We regularly went to have meals with Israeli families in the settlement, and I was always very impressed by the mutual aid that prevailed. The spirit of solidarity was strong. As for France, it seemed very far away. Among my friends, we hardly ever spoke of it. Implicitly, we had all made the decision to settle in Israel.

At Paratrooper School

As I mentioned before, I requested Israeli citizenship at the end of my stay on the kibbutz. After spending a year at the yeshiva it was now time for me to fulfill my civic duties. So I left to do my military service with the Paratroopers Brigade as a simple soldier. And it was—forgive me the expression—the pits! I realized that up to then I had lived in a cocoon.

We began with six months of basic training. We were confronted with all manner of situations, each more trying than the last. At night we slept on the ground in the rain. We walked without stopping from six in the evening to six in the morning. We were woken up in the middle of the night to go running and showered in the dark when we got back. We learned how to run in the sand with our gear. The officers ran with us, even ahead of us, and they taught us to develop incredible willpower. Thanks to them, I discovered that I was capable of drawing upon unimagined psychological resources—so much so that, during those long months, I never once feared myself unequal to the task. In fact, the only thing I was afraid of was not understanding the orders of the officers, who spoke Hebrew at full speed. This training shaped wills and sealed friendships. I came to know nonreligious Israelis for the first time. In the face of difficulties, we came together.

In the month of December, at the end of basic training, we were sent to Bethlehem to monitor Midnight Mass. At the time, Bethlehem was under Israeli authority, so the Israelis had to ensure security. We arrived three days before to clean out the souk (marketplace). We arrested Arabs. It was not exactly the sweet Christmas atmosphere that I had known as a kid. But when I saw Bethlehem with its decorations I was completely amazed—ecstatic—and I started feeling my old desire to be Christian. During the Mass, we were posted on the rooftops in Tzahal (Israeli Army) uniforms, weapons in hand. So I, in the middle of the night, was watching the basilica below, where the Mass of the Nativity was taking place. I found it enormously difficult to concentrate on my mission. I had only one desire: to drop my rifle and to join all these Christians, to experience Christmas Mass with them. I knew that this desire was completely unreasonable, but it was so strong and so difficult to resist!

When we returned to the base the following evening, I was still completely turned upside down by the strong feelings that had come over me at Bethlehem. However, the context was so different there that I quickly began to think of other things. As soon as basic training was finished, relations with the officers began to change. They got on our case a lot less. In fact, their authority became almost paternal. We started to form real relationships. Among other things, while talking with my sergeant, I realized that he was the brother of the English girl I had dated at the ulpan two years before. What a coincidence!

Then we had to complete three months of intense training intended to prepare us for war. This was in 1984; Lebanon was waiting for us. We trained with real bullets in a simulated battle zone, usually in the middle of the night in order to intensify the hardship. Israeli soldiers were deployed everywhere: in front *and* behind. Mannequins representing the enemy that we had to shoot were arranged in the middle. It was crucial to understand the

orders correctly so as not to kill a classmate. One especially rigorous part of training stayed with me for a long
time. We spent a whole night on the Golan Heights,
in the north of Israel at the Syrian border, awaiting the
order to attack. It froze, and we took turns sleeping. In
the end, the military exercise did not begin until the
following morning.

In the course of those long months spent in the army,
I always wore my kippah under my helmet. The army
gave us time for prayer, and usually we were given a day's
leave for Shabbat. When we were on duty on the Sabbath,
there was no training. On the other hand, we had to carry
our weapons, even though under normal circumstances
we were not supposed to carry anything on the Sabbath.
However, we also had a special Shabbat meal. In Israel it is
a day set apart even for the nonreligious.

Spring arrived. As planned, we took off in a military
truck for the north of Israel, the region of historical Galilee,
very close to the Lebanese and Syrian borders (which is
even today regularly targeted by Hezbollah rocket fire).
Afterward another truck brought us to a camp at the
border. The closer we got, the more my anxiety grew.
I could feel it overwhelming me. I did not feel well. It
was hitting me that I was leaving for war, that I might kill
people or be killed. Images of my family came to the front
of my mind. Did I regret anything? No, nothing at all. I
did not even pray. Suddenly, I felt a great determination
within me. I had to go, so I was going!

I would stay two months in Lebanon—two months that
wound up going fairly smoothly. We were looking for
terrorists and forcibly taking over shepherds' homes in the
fields. Thanks be to God we never had cause to shoot.
Moreover, we were welcomed like heroes when we
arrived in villages in southern Lebanon. The populations

applauded us. Since we were looking for weapons stashed in homes, we entered the homes of Christian families who offered us tea. And there, incredibly, when I saw the icons, my desire for Christ came over me again. I so wanted to talk with the inhabitants and share my attraction to Christ. But it was impossible; I was not allowed to open my mouth. Only the colonel spoke.

On June 10, 1985, my birthday, we left Lebanon. Yet while we were stationed in the north, the situation intensified. Terrorists had penetrated into Israel. We were sent to set up an ambush for them; the truck we got into had the radio on, and we could hear artillery firing. That time I began to pray. Once again I felt intense anxiety, but it decreased in a few moments. I had never felt so close to death. Images from my childhood came back to me. I prayed with all my strength. When I got out of the truck and saw the colonel marching ahead of us, I was not thinking of anything anymore; I just followed him. I was not afraid anymore. Seeing an officer leading the way gives you confidence—it gives you wings. During the night we set up the ambush. Taking turns with infrared binoculars, we surveyed the terrain, trying to detect terrorists. That night another group captured them.

At the end of my year of military service, my officers suggested that I sign up to become a professional and rise through the ranks. I had never imagined my future along those lines, but I did not immediately refuse. I took some time for reflection first, thinking over the intense moments I had experienced with the army. I would never regret those last months, especially because of the very close relationships that had developed. In those months I had learned that for people together in extreme circumstances, religious or political conflicts disappear. Everything that separates them disappears. Every person is important. All the members of a unit support each other. For example, I will never forget what happened in a minefield in Lebanon. A soldier from my squadron who was walking in front hit a landmine. Immediately the doctor rushed into the field to bring him help, without thinking for a second about the danger he was exposing himself to. I was dumbfounded—a man rushes in to save another man without concern for his own life. This, too, is what an individual is capable of. This is what those months in the army taught me.

Before returning to the yeshiva, I decided to take a few weeks' vacation. But I had absolutely no desire to return to France. The more time went on, the more I told myself there was nothing left for me there. My little brother came for a visit. What a joy it was to see him after all that time. We travelled from Tiberias to Eilat. Then, since I had no apartment or family, we went back to the kibbutz together. After working there for a while, we took off again for the seashore at Tel Aviv. It was so nice, after a year in the army, to be in shorts and a tee shirt again.

Throughout that year, my girlfriend D. was living in Jerusalem learning Japanese. After my brother left, we finally saw each other again. A short time later she decided to go live in the territories because housing was less expensive there. We remained in contact by telephone for a year. It was only when I went over to the ultra-Orthodox religious world that our love affair came to an end.

An Ultra-Orthodox Jew

With the end of my military service the three-year program was finished. So I had to make a decision: whether or not to return to France. To tell the truth I had already decided a long time before: I was staying in Israel! To start with, I returned to my yeshiva for religious Zionists at Kiryat Arba. But I very quickly realized that I no longer felt at home there. From then on I was really aspiring to something more spiritual. I desired to grow closer to God.

The following year, 1986, I returned to France for the summer. In Paris I made the acquaintance of a dentist who quickly became a friend. He was an ultra-Orthodox Jew. We talked at length and he introduced me to his spirituality. He even took me to attend a rabbi's class. I was very interested in this new approach—so much so that when I returned to my yeshiva, I no longer agreed with the ideas taught there. I began to question the Zionist ideal. Among other things, I no longer spoke of Israel but of Ha Aretz, which means "the Land", or Ha Aretz Ha Kodesh, "the Holy Land". My appearance also changed: I gave up jeans and dress shirts in favor of black slacks, a white dress shirt, a jacket, and a hat. By wearing those different clothes, I wanted to mark a break so as to enter into a way of life more radically centered on God.

Without talking about it to just anyone, I also began to look for an ultra-Orthodox kibbutz or moshav. (A moshav is a collective where everyone has a house and works, either on site—for example, in agriculture, viticulture, or

animal farming—or off site, with the money earned redis-
tributed among the families according to their needs.)
To this end I travelled around the country whenever I
had the opportunity. My dedication would pay off: in
the month of December, during the Hanukkah holidays,
I found a moshav and went to meet the man in charge.
Unfortunately, he explained that since it was winter
there was no work for me. My disappointment did not
last long since he suggested an ultra-Orthodox yeshiva
in Israel, at Bnei Brak. I settled there at the beginning of
the year 1987.

Let me make a few clarifications about the difference
between religious Zionists and the ultra-Orthodox. The
religious Zionist movement, founded by Rav Kook, who
came from Russia, sought to create a religious Jewish state
in Israel. The ultra-Orthodox, on the other hand, were
not in favor of a Jewish state or of the reconquest of Israel
by force. They thought that God had exiled the Jewish
people because of their errors and that He would lead
them back to the Holy Land with the Messiah. Thus they
were opposed to the use of violence for the expansion
of territory. At the beginning, they did not wish to be
involved in society, political life, or the army. Today,
however, they have two parties in the Knesset—the
Banner of the Torah for the Ashkenazi ultra-Orthodox
and the Shas for the Sephardic ultra-Orthodox. Their aim
is not so much to involve themselves in the affairs of the
state as to defend their distinctiveness. In effect they hold
a unique status and live as an autarchy. Their way of life is
fairly radical: they dedicate themselves to God alone. They
do not have televisions, for example.

At Bnei Brak, we lived like monks. I was an intern and
studied all day long. For Jews, study is its own reward.
One studies to study because as a student one sanctifies and

protects the Hebrew people, and through them, one saves and protects the world.

The day began at seven with prayer. Then we would begin study, which lasted until evening. In the morning, study was divided into three periods. First, we sat in pairs, one person facing the other, studying a theme through a text from the Talmud. Then the rabbi gave his lecture. Though it was a lecture, if one of us disagreed he could challenge what he said, interrupting in the middle of his lecture and provoking a discussion (which is unthinkable for the French). There is a Jewish saying on this subject, which goes: "I learned some from my masters, a lot from my friends, and even more from my students." Finally, we would break into pairs again and review the text in light of what the rabbi said. In this way we reviewed and learned it. The afternoon was more relaxed: we read the Talmud quickly, alone or in pairs. Finally, in the evening we would study a book by a great author such as Maimonides or Nahmanides.

There, developing my knowledge of the Talmud, I was preparing to make a horrible discovery that was to torture me for years, even after my baptism. I recognized that Jesus was treated in several passages of the Talmud. Each time, my heart would beat faster and my attention would grow tense. And then, I would be dumbfounded: Jesus, my Beloved, to whom I had spoken secretly since childhood and to whom I was so attracted, the same Jesus was called a blasphemer. Even worse, I learned that it was forbidden to pronounce His name! The Talmud is the teaching of the wise men of Israel, and the wise men of Israel have an absolute authority. How could I question what was written? I had *no* right to do so. You can imagine the violence of the conflict that was going on inside of me. And it did not stop there: I realized that the story of Jesus and Mary such as it was presented by the Talmud had absolutely nothing to do with the story recounted in the Gospels I had read as a teenager. And it was not just a difference of point of view. It was clear that one of the two was lying in its account of the facts.

From the yeshiva I could see the church of Jaffa, which was topped with a crucifix. And as soon as I saw a cross, nothing could be done; my attraction to Jesus would start all over again. I was literally captive. And yet I fought against it. I tried to resist with all my strength and to reason with myself. I told myself again and again that this desire was impure and that it was aroused by the devil to make me stumble. But this attraction to the cross was stronger than I. I suffered. I was wracked with guilt and remorse.

For religious Jews, Jesus is the devil. For this reason I am rather skeptical about the sincerity of Jewish-Christian dialogue such as it is practiced (even if in substance it can be very rich). For me at any rate, I can tell you that when I was an Orthodox Jew, I would have had—forgive me the expression—absolutely *nothing* to do with Christians. There is no question that dialogue is better than beating each other up. But if the exchange passes over in silence what is contentious, it serves no purpose. In dialogue, each participant, Christian as well as Jew, must stand up for what he believes and not betray himself in order to please or to be appealing to the other. If the Christians are afraid of talking about Jesus, it is no longer an exchange. Each party must respect the other in what he is and what he believes, but without being ashamed to speak to his own experience.

Though I had entered the ultra-Orthodox world in order to grow closer to God, in the end I was so absorbed in study that I lost the spontaneous relationship I previously had with Him. It was only when I went out on the street that I would go back to talking to Him. Study is a good thing, but it must be understood as Saint Thomas Aquinas understood it: each time that he came up against a theological problem, he would fly to the Blessed Sacrament, stop his reflection, put himself in the Real Presence of God, and ask Him to explain what he did not understand. At the end of his life, Saint Thomas had a very profound mystical experience during which Jesus told him: "You have spoken well of me, Thomas." Yet afterward Saint Thomas affirmed that, compared to his direct experience of God, everything he had written—his *Summa Theologica*— was so much straw. The goal of studies is only to lead to God, to know Him better in order to love Him better and therefore to love His creatures better.

Moreover, Jewish prayers are so codified that there is no place for spontaneous prayer—except incorporated into the nineteen blessings, the central prayer of the Jewish liturgy. Even though the Jewish Scriptures abound with texts that speak of meditation, in reality meditation is practiced very little. At any rate, meditation is not mental prayer—that form of prayer that is an interior dialogue with God. In mental prayer, our soul speaks freely to Him and He speaks to us (even if not always explicitly). What is called mental prayer in the Catholic world does not exist in the Jewish world. There is no filial relationship, no simple heart-to-heart with God. A Jew could never say what a peasant said to the Curé d'Ars about his prayer: "I look at Him and He looks at me." I am familiar with one exception, the Breslov Jews, who go out into the forest at midnight to talk with God. But the Breslovers are marginalized, even if their founder, Rabbi Nachman (1772–1810), is recognized.

At the age of twenty-three, when my studies were drawing to a close, I began feeling the desire to start a

An Ultra-Orthodox Jew   59

family. You have to know that in Judaism a man can be sanctified only through marriage. It is the only religious vocation possible. The marriage process, based on the Law given by God to Moses, is codified. During the first period, the rabbi organizes a *shidduch* (matchmaking meeting) to introduce two young people who are looking to marry and who have already given him a few criteria. The meeting follows strict rules: the young people are not allowed to meet alone or to touch one another, even by handshake. Thus one of the rabbis I was close to at my yeshiva contacted the director of an ultra-Orthodox girls' seminary and, shortly after, I was invited to come to a married couple's apartment in Jerusalem where the young woman would be waiting for me. We sat down in the living room to talk while the couple stayed in the adjoining room. We talked about our studies, our desires for a family, and our goals in life. The whole thing was very interesting, but I was not attracted to her. She was short and a little chubby—in other words, *not* my type. We said goodbye to each other, and I gave a report to my rabbi. He set to work looking for another young woman and organized a second meeting. Unfortunately, that time, *I* was the one who did not appeal to the girl.

During the almost two years that I spent at the ultra-Orthodox yeshiva, I succeeded in avoiding the annual month of military service in the Miluim (Army Reserve), which is required in Israel. However, it was not to last; the military authorities wound up finding me. That was one of the reasons my rabbi decided to send me back to France. In effect, the ultra-Orthodox do not want to serve in the army. They hold that the study of the Torah, to which they dedicate their lives, protects those in the military. This is the principle of social division as it existed in France in the Middle Ages. In 1948 there was an agreement on this topic between the great ultra-Orthodox rabbi Chazon Ish and Prime Minister Ben-Gurion although it has been debated off and on ever since.

In 1989, after I had just completed five years of full-time formation, not counting my year at the kibbutz, the plan was for me to continue my rabbinical formation for one more year at Aix-les-Bains in France. When I left Israel, I did not have a university degree (because a yeshiva is not a university), but I had a certificate given by three rabbis. In Judaism, the authority of a three-person tribunal is recognized. Thus a degree granted by three ultra-Orthodox rabbis is juridically valid. The certificate allowed me to be a rabbi. The way the system works is that to be a rabbi in France you need either a degree recognized by the Central Consistory of the French government or a certificate from the ultra-Orthodox or the Chabad-Lubavitch (Orthodox Jewish, Hasidic movement), whose very rigorous and thorough teachings are prized. I could just as easily teach in the Consistory network as in ultra-Orthodox and Lubavitcher communities. The Reform Jews, the Liberals, and the Mizrahi have their own networks.

Back to France with a Hat and a Beard

What a disappointment! There I was taking a plane to Paris in spite of myself—I who had planned to spend my whole life in Israel. I did try, however, to see the good side of things. I was fortunate to have in my pocket the certificate authenticating the first part of my rabbinical studies. Thanks to that certificate, I would be able to teach at last, and that was all that mattered.

When I arrived in Paris, I first went to my parents' home. What culture shock! Just imagine: I had left home dressed as a teenager and came back with a hat, a beard, a dark suit, and a white dress shirt. Unremarkable in Israel, but not in La Courneuve. I refused to hug my sisters because the only women ultra-Orthodox men hug are their wives, and even then, not in public. I felt like an extraterrestrial. I explained to my parents that I wanted to go to Aix-les-Bains to enter a respected rabbinical school to complete my studies. Since they were already reluctant about the idea of my becoming a rabbi, an ultra-Orthodox rabbi no less, that was quite a blow. My big brother was shocked. I felt uneasy and stayed only a few days. With hindsight, I can see that there is a kind of secular fundamentalism in France. The secularist cannot accept that someone might have motivations in life other than his own. It is true that, for my part, I would not respect my sister's choice when she married an Armenian, which she would greatly resent. I understand her feelings, but I could not support her marrying a non-Jew. For that matter, neither could my mother, who justified her opposition to the marriage by recalling that her mother-in-law was opposed to her son's marriage to a Spanish Catholic (the uncle we visited when I was a kid), before finally accepting it much later.

When I arrived at my parents' home, I did not find my room or the view of Sacré-Cœur. What had happened was that while I was in Israel our housing block had been destroyed and my family had changed apartments. It was only the next day, as I went in to Paris to teach a class, that I saw the basilica again from afar, upon arriving at the Gare du Nord. But I looked at it as if it were a postcard. There was a screen between us.

As planned, I then went to the Aix-les-Bains yeshiva, one of France's principal ultra-Orthodox talmudic academies. I lived in a ghetto there. One evening around midnight in the study room, while I was reading a text by a Lubavitcher rabbi, one of the men in charge who had seen a light on came in and looked at me suspiciously:

"Are you a Lubavitcher?"

"No.... But one can read a commentary written by a Lubavitcher rabbi without being a Lubavitcher!"

"Hmm ..."

That did not seem to placate him. To tell the truth, I was more and more interested in the Lubavitcher scientific mystical theology—you could even say philosophy. Already, at Bnei Brak in Israel, I had secretly read the Tanya, a mystical treatise whose reading the ultra-Orthodox categorically forbid. I did not feel free at the Aix-les-Bains yeshiva. They made it clear to me that if I continued down that path, I would not finish my studies or find a wife. One day, I met up with a rabbi who had left my yeshiva to found a center for Lubavitcher studies outside of Paris. He advised me to marry and to come join him.

A Lubavitcher Jew

That was how, following his advice, I left yeshiva in Aix-les-Bains to settle in Grenoble. There, I taught in a school whose male and female principals were Lubavitcher. In the evenings, I gave classes for adults. I also helped the rabbi attached to the synagogue—as an assistant priest helps the parish priest. Thanks to my rabbinical office and the certificate granted by my yeshiva, I could fill in for him in the liturgy, the reading of the Torah, and other capacities. I realized that being a rabbi is in the end only an office and not necessarily a calling from God. It is not the same thing as for Catholic priests. This realization would play a big part in the decision I would later make to settle in the Paris suburbs rather than elsewhere in the country where I could be a rabbi in a synagogue. During that time I also pursued close study of Jewish mysticism. God was undoubtedly laying the groundwork for a rebirth of my intimate relationship with Jesus.

One day I was invited to the installation of the consistorial rabbi of Grenoble by the chief rabbi of France at the time. All the religious personalities of the city were gathered there, including a Protestant pastor and a parish priest. During the ceremony, I tried to concentrate on what the rabbi was saying, but I did not succeed. I was completely distracted by the priest, whom I recognized by his Roman collar. I saw only him and had only one objective: to go talk to him. Obviously, with my long beard and my hat, I did not permit myself to go meet him. Once more I experienced real heartbreak: a struggle between my heart's deep desire, over which I had no control, and my reason, which was struggling to come out on top. I left the ceremony extremely frustrated. I felt as though I were living through a tragedy worse than *Romeo and Juliet*! I was supposed to despise Christ, who was an object of scandal for my people, but I could not keep myself from loving Him.

I got along well with the principal and his wife. We had some very good times together. For the feast of Hanukkah in the month of December, they sent me to ski resorts to "evangelize" Jews. This was the method: we would walk two by two trying to recognize Jews. Then we would go up to them and ask if they had lit Hanukkah candles. If they responded in the negative, we would give them candles. We were truly very well received by the people, and there were some wonderful experiences. Once more, however, I was not indifferent to the Christmas decorations in these little mountain villages. Each time, they aroused even more my attraction to Jesus and my sense of guilt.

Moreover, every time I walked through the city of Grenoble, with its pedestrian thoroughfares and its churches, I felt filled with love for Christ. An irrepressible desire to go into a church would rise within me, as it had when I was a child. When it was happening, I had no guilty conscience. But what I experienced inside before and after was terrible. In the end, I never acted on my desire, not because of the great guilt I felt but because I was very afraid of being caught by my coreligionists. If a Christian enters a synagogue, no other Christian reproaches him. On the other hand, according to Jewish Law, it is formally forbidden to enter a church.

Meeting My Wife

As I explained before, in the Jewish community holiness comes through marriage. Consequently, when Jews notice young people who are unmarried, they organize meetings: the famous shidduchim. Beforehand, they ask the young people involved what kind of profile appeals to them, including the physical side of things; it is all *very* pragmatic. Then they consult their files and organize meetings for persons whose requests match. Let me be clear: nothing is set in stone. There is no forced marriage. Even girls can continue their studies before marrying if they prefer. Since I had not met the woman who would become my wife at the two shidduchim that were organized for me in Israel, I persisted. This time I asked the principal of the school in Grenoble where I was teaching to take care of finding me a bride.

The young woman he selected for me was a Lubavitcher from a Sephardic family in Lyon. She had previously worked as a kindergarten teacher in the same school in Grenoble but left when I arrived to study in a seminary for women in the Paris area. Our first interaction was over the telephone. Then we called each other once a week. Next, since we were getting along well, we decided to meet during school vacation. That was how we began to meet regularly in a café, always in public. During those dates, we talked about what we wanted to do in life. It went on like that for a year while we took the time to reflect. Finally, we decided to get married.

My fiancé was named Martine. I found her very attractive, and we shared the same views. We both had the same passion for the mystical texts of Hasidic thought. Plus, she was all right with my continuing to study as I had hoped to do. And above all, we both wanted to have a big family. I had always wanted to have children. And the very warm Israeli families I had known during my studies in Israel had reinforced this desire. They also introduced me to a kind of family life that was very different from what I had known as a child. Since ultra-Orthodox and Lubavitcher Jews do not have television, the family is centered on life with God. The father asks his children: "How did you understand this Word of God? How did you live your week with your friends?" At the dinner table, talk centers on assessing how you are living out your religion from day to day and how you are living, period. There was no comparison with what I had known in my parents' home. We had spoken only of exterior topics: politics, war, football.

To celebrate our engagement, the principal at Martine's school wanted to host a party with her colleagues and students. However, the custom is for the engagement party to happen at the home of the future bridegroom; for that reason my mother absolutely insisted on organizing the reception at *her* home. Since Martine was a little annoyed, she asked my mother if she could invite her colleagues and friends. My mother answered: "No, I'd rather not; it might be too noisy." In my opinion, she simply did not want a boatload of Lubavitcher Jews coming into her home. In the end, our engagement party took place in two parts: in the afternoon at my parents' place with the family and a few very close friends, and in the evening at my future wife's school.

I think that at heart my mother was angry with me. She had not been happy about my leaving for Israel against her wishes. My parents had never come to see me while I was there, allegedly because they did not have the money for the trip. They had, however, gone to visit my brother in the Canary Islands. Later, my brothers and sisters would reproach me for having cut myself off from the family and for having appeared ungrateful toward my mother after everything she had done for me when I was a child. In fact, my mother, while not exactly tender, was possessive. Sad to say, my relations with my mother were far from serene. Be that as it may, her misunderstanding with my wife did not intervene in our marital relationship, as can sometimes be the case; I had already distanced myself from her influence by becoming religious and then by going to live in Israel.

The day of our wedding arrived. It was in the month of July 1990; I was twenty-six. For the reception, we had rented a school hall. Since I really liked dancing, we hired an orchestra and consequently wanted a large space at our disposal. The religious ceremony took place in the courtyard. Our families and friends were all gathered around us. Following the tradition, while the rabbi spoke the seven ritual blessings, Martine and I were under the chuppah, the wedding canopy. Afterward, the party started. A large sheet divided the room into two parts since men and women are not supposed to mix for reasons of purity. The orchestra played only Jewish religious music, Middle Eastern or Hasidic, and we danced until two in the morning. It was a very joyful party. My father, brothers, cousins, and uncles, who had never seen a wedding like it, were enchanted.

Let me say a short word on music. In the Jewish world, there is not a time and a place for profane things and another for God. Each instant is lived with God. (By the way, I have trouble finding the equivalent to this in the lay Catholic world.) Consequently, when I became Orthodox, I no longer listened to anything but religious music. Fortunately, there is Jewish music for every taste, mood, and moment in life.

The director of my ultra-Orthodox yeshiva in Bnei Brak came to our wedding. He had come all the way from Israel. Nevertheless, he did not look too kindly on my marrying a Lubavitcher. Let me say a few words about what distinguishes and divides ultra-Orthodox and Lubavitcher Jews. Lubavitcher Jews belong to a branch of Judaism that grew out of the Hasidic philosophic school. The founder of this branch, born in Russia in the middle of the eighteenth century, Baal Shem Tov, wanted to make Jewish mysticism, which until then had been reserved to a few initiates, accessible to everyone, even the most humble. He and his disciples submitted to the light of reason the notions developed by Kabbalah in the Zohar, the great work of mystical exegesis of the Torah—the true Jewish mysticism, not the New Age mysticism that gets dished out today. As far as the practice of the Law goes, ultra-Orthodox and Lubavitcher Jews have the same doctrine. But the ultra-Orthodox are more centered on morality. They emphasize texts that say what must be done or avoided—the texts that insist on the danger of evil, on the fear of God. According to them, interest in mysticism should not begin before the age of forty. The Hasidic texts, on the other hand, try to think about the mystery of God through his Creation, through human beings, and through the Scriptures. They are centered on wonder before the greatness of God, who has created the world ex nihilo. They meditate on lines of Scripture like this one: "For ever, O LORD, your word is firmly fixed in the heavens" (Ps 119:89). What does that mean? This questioning leads to a meditative state but not yet the dialogue with God that is Christian mental prayer, as I underlined before. In reality, the Lubavitcher Jews that I knew were not especially mystical. But at that time, I was discovering a fascinating intellectual world.

Renting in Galilee

As Martine and I had agreed, for the first two years of our marriage I resumed my rabbinical studies at a Lubavitcher yeshiva in the Essonne. Then, since I still wanted to deepen my knowledge of Jewish mysticism, we decided to return to Israel—or rather, only I was *returning* to Israel, because my wife had never lived there before. We settled at Safed, the major center for religious studies of texts from the first centuries of our era in the Kabbalistic tradition. The city of Safed is located in the mountains in the north of the country, in Galilee. We rented a small suburban house overlooking Lake Tiberias. It was gorgeous! I studied in a *kollel*, a rabbinical school for married people. As for my wife, she was enrolled at the ulpan to learn Hebrew and to get to know the country. The two of us regularly went swimming in Haifa along a natural beach that the tourists did not know about.

Everything was going well until the day the army found me. This is the KGB side of Israel. One day I received a summons to fulfill my duty to the Miluim, which I had avoided by returning to France four years earlier. That time I went to my appointment; from there, I was immediately sent off without even being allowed to tell Martine that I was not coming home. That is how it happens over there: they do not waste *any* time. Two days later, I could at last telephone her. Obviously, she was enormously worried. I was brought to a prison located in the occupied territories to watch over the prisoners. At the end of a week, I was entitled to a day's leave. At one in the morning, I rang the doorbell at our house in military dress without having been able to alert my wife that I was coming home. She was in quite a state. Those incidents took a toll on her patience. She told me that she was not enjoying herself in Safed and that she wanted to return to France.

I perfectly understood her reaction. She was a Western woman, she was alone in Safed without family, and she did not speak the language. But for me, to tell the truth, I was not all that upset at having been requisitioned by the army without warning. I was even enjoying myself at times. For in the course of a few weeks in the group I landed in, I began rediscovering that quality of human relations that I had so appreciated in the army. One Sabbath day, I began to sing religious chants from the top of the tower where I was keeping watch. When I came back down, the other soldiers, none of whom were religious, questioned me. They had heard me. So I undertook to teach them the Shabbat chants, and we all began to sing together! That was my little missionary side, afraid of nothing. After that episode the general, an Iraqi Jew who was not at all observant, had me brought in and called to order; it was forbidden to proselytize in the army ranks. However, immediately afterward, he congratulated me on having instilled vitality in the team. He seemed totally happy!

Strangely enough there are many virtues to military service. You appreciate life better after living through dangerous situations. When you return to civilian life, you appreciate the very fact that you are healthy, little things amaze you, and you feel everything more intensely. The army also instills a discipline that strengthens the will. During service you have to perform tasks you have no desire to do. Well, I have to say that this forms character, especially in our day when as young people we tend to want to do only what we feel like doing.

As I was saying, my wife was not at all happy with this military interlude—to such a degree that after eighteen months in Safed, we decided to return to France. For me this return to France was a sacrifice. Nevertheless, I loved my wife, and I wanted her to be happy. Two days before our departure, I began to cry secretly in a corner. I was viscerally attached to the Holy Land. I felt in my element in the heart of that Mediterranean Israeli society. In that little country you go from one landscape and climate to another in less than an hour, the weather is warm, and the quality of life is much better.

So once again I was returning to France against my wishes. But with hindsight I am convinced that it was divine Providence that wished it so, because it was then that my desire for Jesus was going to come back bigger than ever underneath my beard, my hat, and my strict Jewish orthodoxy.

One, Two, Three ... Seven Children

So there we were back in France. We settled in the Paris region. I taught part-time in a Jewish school while continuing my rabbinical studies part-time in a kollel in Paris. Yes, I was still studying all the time. That might appear surprising but in fact there is nothing extraordinary about it. For in Judaism study of the Torah is so vital that the community pays men, even men with very busy professional lives, to continue to perfect their knowledge of the Torah. All observant Jews are thus formed to pass on the Torah. A Jewish man might very well work in a business and be a rabbi. The rabbi manages the synagogue, leads prayer, gives sermons—but he can also delegate these tasks to the faithful.

For her part, my wife returned to her work as a teacher in a Jewish school. The more time went by, the more worried she was about not yet having a baby. In Judaism, as can be seen in the Bible, expecting a baby is a sign of blessing and thus a way of obtaining the community's recognition. Consequently, if children are slow in coming, the stakes are not only emotional. So she decided to undergo medical tests. The results were reassuring: everything was fine. And as it happened, the children came in good time.

They were born very quickly, one after another: Rachel in 1994, Déborah in 1995, Rivka (Rebecca) in 1996, Myriam in 1997, Youssef (Raphaël) in 1999, Menahem (Gabriel) in 2001, and Chneor (Louis) in 2003. What joy!

My wife wanted a big family and so did I. However, after the birth of Myriam I suggested that we take a break. I very much wanted to have a boy, but it seemed to me that for the good of our marriage and our four daughters, it would be better to wait a little. But my wife was not of the same opinion!

When Rachel was born my wife stopped working. From that time on, I worked full-time to meet the needs of the family, and I also gave classes to adults. Despite all the work, I was present for and very close to my children. Their blossoming and education were very important to me. I had a special relationship with each one. I loved playing with them, bringing them to the park and to La Courneuve, and teaching them how to ride a bike. My wife took care of their daily education and homework. It goes without saying that after having taken care of the kids, we did not have much time to spend alone with each other. Fortunately we had neither a television nor the Internet. Whenever I found a free moment, I continued to study Jewish mystical theology about the Word of God.

I did my part for the life of the household. I was charged with the provisioning, and I have to say that it was a real pain in the neck! For some of the shopping had to be done in Jewish shops and some in non-Jewish shops. Sunday morning, after prayer at the synagogue, I would take the bus to go to the kosher shops in Paris with the caddy and buy everything an Orthodox Jewish family must eat kosher: meat, cheese and all dairy products, crackers, wine, alcohol, grape juice, etc.—all of it in large supply, of course. On the return trip, I would be burdened like a camel. Everything else—cleaning supplies, diapers, water, soap, etc.—I would buy in a supermarket on a weekday evening. I was also in charge of buying clothes for the children, sometimes alone, sometimes with my wife.

My wife and I had few areas of disagreement. Nevertheless, she was more scrupulous than I concerning the application of the Law. For example, after not having gone on vacation for three summers, it so happened that I brought the kids to the beach. We went round-trip to Trouville for the day. My wife did *not* at all approve. Indeed, for Orthodox Jews, the beach is an impure place because the people are undressed. Among other things, this event gave rise to a mini-scandal. One day, some people from the Lubavitcher community came to find me:

"You really have no scruple about going to the beach, and with your children no less?"

Surprised, I retorted:

"You know, during the summer in Paris, a woman wearing a tight-fitting outfit is more distracting than a woman in a bathing suit!"

"In Paris, it's different. You're preoccupied with what you're doing: classes or shopping!"

"And you really believe that at the beach I'm not preoccupied with all my kids? You really think I have time to play Casanova and check out the ladies?"

To me their arguments were unreasonable. When I had in mind to do something that I really did not see any evil in, I was not going to let others dictate my behavior. Above all I was thinking of my children's well-being. They were so happy to go to the beach and breathe the fresh air, and for that matter, so was I. But my wife never came. She respected the Law at any cost.

We also disagreed over the television. I had bought one so that the kids could watch animated videos. But my wife was upset because she disapproved of videos depicting impure animals. So after that I was careful with my selection so as not to shock her, though to my mind watching the "Three Little Pigs" was hardly criminal.

On the other hand, when there was talk of us all going to the mountains for vacation, we were in complete agreement. The mountains, those are kosher! So much so that the Lubavitcher community organizes a big seminary in the Alps every year and brings along a kosher grocery, making our life a lot easier. I loved those summer vacations with my family. It was my opportunity to show the children the beauty of nature that God created. We played, we laughed, we gazed at the sky and the stars. It was wonderful!

A Double Life

I want to take a step back to the period before the children were born, when we had just returned to France. As I mentioned earlier, at that moment my "Christ syndrome" came back stronger than ever—and thus, so did my interior struggle. I told myself that all these feelings were coming back to attack me because France was an impure country. I would *so* much have preferred staying in Safed and living in the mountains. Things were so much simpler for me there. I was immersed in Hasidism, the Jewish mystical theology. In that tradition I had discovered another universe and spent a great deal of time meditating. But upon my return to France, my desire for Jesus was irresistible, stronger than I was: I returned to church and started receiving Communion again. It had been so long since I had crossed the threshold of a church. Now I was returning to Sacré-Cœur with my rabbi's beard. Just imagine what it looked like. I purchased a cross again and started wearing it under my clothes. I also began reading Saint John's Gospel again, learning it by heart. It was safer that way: at least, in my head, no one would be able to find it.

This religious double life may appear shocking. It was true; I was carrying two identities inside myself. But it was more like a spiritual struggle than duplicity or betrayal. How was it possible to live out these two identities at the same time? I did not know. But I lived with them both, and strangely I did not feel guilty. Until our children were born I had enough time to slip away to some isolated spot

now and again in order to contemplate my crucifix, especially during our vacations in the countryside. I would go
off for a walk, hide in the forest or around the bend of the
trail, set my cross on a tree, and contemplate it. I did not
question what I was doing. At any rate, it was better not to.
I prayed to Jesus, who is God. On the other hand, I found
it difficult to say the Our Father because I was gripped by
the feeling I was betraying the God of the Torah.

I did not talk to my wife about this struggle playing
out inside of me. And she had absolutely no suspicion. It
was not that I wanted to conceal my history with Jesus
from her, but rather that I knew she would not understand. When the Jews learned that the rabbi Saul, perse-
cutor of Christians, had been converted to Christ, they
did not try to learn why. They did not even ask him to
explain himself. They immediately wanted to kill him
because he was guilty of betrayal: either he had turned
into a dangerous blasphemer, or he had lost his head. For
Orthodox Jews, Christians are impure. This is why it was
not even thinkable that I should speak to my wife about
it all. But believe me, keeping this secret to myself was far
from easy. You can imagine my crisis of conscience.

Of course, it would have been comforting to unburden
myself to someone. But who was there? A rabbi? What
good could come of it; I already knew what he would tell
me. A priest, then? One day, while we were on vacation
with my wife's family around Lyon, I got up early and left
for the city. I went into a church and attended Mass. At
the end, I went to find the priest. He was a Dominican.
We started to talk, and I let it all out. I told him everything: my life as an Orthodox Jew, my attraction to Christ.
He listened and suggested I come to see him when I was
back in Paris, where he lived too. So when I got back from
vacation I went to his home. After the first visit, he would

come to my home once a week on Wednesday evenings while my wife was attending her religion class. We talked about God. He asked me to find him a translation of a midrash, a collection of Jewish exegeses of the Scriptures, and he gave me one of his books about Noah. He always left before my wife came back. I found him very kind. But these clandestine meetings would not last long. As it happened, our apartment was broken into shortly after. The break-in happened during the day. When my wife got home that evening, she found the apartment turned upside down. And there in the mess she discovered the Dominican father's book, my cross, and the Gospels! By the time I came home myself, she was absolutely furious. She screamed: "You've gone crazy! You must throw everything out—these are impure things!"

It may seem surprising that she did not try to learn more about it all. But we Orthodox Jews are educated not to want to understand the phenomenon of conversion to Christianity and to react against it violently. You should know that a converted Jew goes in front of a tribunal that declares him an apostate. In our daily prayer, the prayer structuring our lives, we pronounce a curse on these apostate Jews. Among other things, Maimonides, the great Andalusian rabbi from the twelfth century, one of the most important figures of Judaism and one of the most esteemed by non-Jews—Saint Thomas Aquinas nicknamed him the Eagle of the Synagogue—formalized a Jewish credo called the Thirteen Articles—that concludes with this commentary: "He who believes all these fundamental points belongs to the communion of Israel; and it is a precept to love him, to express charity to him, and to observe in his regard everything that God had prescribed between man and his neighbor, even when the strength of the passions leads him to commit sins. But if someone is so perverse as to deny one of these articles of faith, he is outside the communion of Israel, and *it is a precept to hate him and to exterminate him.*"

After her discovery, my wife urged me to see a rabbi. She thought I had lost my head! I would surely have thought the same thing in her place. In any case, I could not explain things to her. The Jewish mentality of today has not changed since Saint Paul. The only thing I could tell her was that it was all totally independent of my will and had begun in my youth. At that time, I suggested divorce to her. I sensed that this love for Jesus was so strong that He would not quit me, and I did not want to make her suffer. But she refused; she loved me. I think she did not speak about it to anyone. Maybe she thought it would go away? I am reminded of a sentence from a talmudic treatise: "God is ready to tear his Name in two in order to establish peace in a married couple." So we decided together to throw out everything: the Gospels, the cross, and the book about Noah. And I did not get back in touch with the Dominican father.

Rachel was born barely one year after this episode, in May 1994. So we moved to a bigger apartment located in the same city. One evening, coming home from work and tired, I felt the need to relax. I turned on the radio and happened upon radio Notre-Dame! I really liked that station and began listening to it in secret whenever I had the chance. However, in time I had had enough of concealing. So I continued to listen to the Catholic station openly. My wife considered it evil. She told me again and again that it was impure, but she let me listen. A little later, I returned to Sacré-Cœur and obtained a photo of the Sacred Heart of Jesus. I would regularly take it out in secret in the dining room, then kneel and place myself in the presence of Christ.

A Kosher Homemaking Father

In July 2002, my mother died. We had not truly reconciled, even though in the last years we had seen each other
regularly and she was close to our children. For me this
was a difficult trial to overcome. I did not know then that
I was about to experience an even more difficult trial. In
the month of December of the same year, when I had
not yet finished grieving for my mother, my wife, then
pregnant with our seventh child, learned that she was ill.

The illness got worse and my wife largely blamed
herself. "I should have listened to you," she told me, "and
spaced out the births." I tried to reassure her: "Your illness
has nothing to do with the children!" When Chneor was
born prematurely, he was put in an incubator while my
wife was cared for in another part of the hospital. I ran
from one to the other, all the while trying to take care
of the six other children as well as possible. I organized
their dispersal among several families from the Jewish
community who had offered to watch them.

My wife died on March 11, 2004. The day before the
doctor told me that my wife's death was imminent. I kept
watch over her all night, from Wednesday evening to
Thursday morning. Then I had to go home to see the
children at the house. When I came back, she was gone!
She had waited for me to leave. I think I do not need
to explain the pain I felt then. Having to go through it
is not something I wish on anyone. I cried a lot. But I
did not think, as Jews say in these situations: "God has

given, God has taken away"—no, not really. Neither did I revolt against God; I have never revolted against God. I trusted in Him. I did not have the time to dwell on my grief. From now on I was the only one responsible for consoling, feeding, and caring for seven children. Rachel was only ten and Chneor, one.

Two months before my wife's death, I asked my sister-in-law to take care of our baby son, Chneor. But my wife explicitly asked me to keep the children with me when she was gone. She entrusted me with their education. (Today, I am proud that our children are well educated, thanks be to God.) She did not want our children to live with members of her family, some of whom had gone away on trips while she was sick. After her death, I wanted Chneor to come back to live with us; but since I would be alone with many young children, my wife's sister offered to keep him for a while, and I accepted. This decision hurt me very deeply, but I was aware that I could not adequately take care of all of the children at the same time.

Y., my childhood Muslim friend, called me on the telephone. He had learned about my wife's death. His call touched me enormously and warmed my heart. He told me: "Remember, we were friends! The friendship hasn't disappeared because we've been apart. Even when the ties are broken, they remain, only invisible! Come visit me in the Canaries!" Unfortunately, even though I really wanted to see him again, I could not respond to his invitation because I was ultra-Orthodox.

So there I was, a full-time homemaker, no doubt with the grace of God. I am also sure that the military training I underwent in Israel served me greatly. I deployed a will and capacities to maintain a household that I would have never suspected I had. I quickly realized that going back to work was unthinkable. Being the father of a kosher family is not a sinecure, and before I had done my part for the life of the household; but now, all of a sudden, I had to manage everything, and that was an entirely different story. I had to learn to do all the cooking, the Shabbat cakes, the bread, etc. That said, I found pleasure in doing these things. Practical, concrete daily life had something magical about it for me, whereas before I had not enjoyed housework. Yet kosher meals require a great deal of planning. Mixing meat and milk is forbidden. You have to have two sets of dishes, one for meat and one for milk, and the two dish sets cannot touch or be washed at the same time. You need two casseroles, two tablecloths, two washbasins, etc. You cannot wash a meat meal in a sink containing the milk dishes. On Fridays, I spent all day in my kitchen, preparing the Shabbat meals. In short, it was not easy. I also had to see to the children's schooling, bring them to the speech therapist, the psychologist, the dentist; I had to do the dishes (we did not have a dishwasher), the ironing, the tons of laundry; there were administrative tasks, shopping, driving the kids to the Jewish school and picking them up when school got out; and finally, above all, being available for them. I also always kept a little time for reading, studying, and praying. I was never discouraged. I did not allow myself to get sick either physically or psychologically. Yet, there were plenty of things to fall apart over. I had no idea how I got through it all—in any case, not with my merely human strength.

Allow me a little tangent on my decision to stop working. I am aware that some did not understand this choice, and consequently the choice to live only on family welfare and long-term unemployment benefits. The people who judged me were undoubtedly ignorant of what it means to take care of and to educate six still young children alone. It is a full-time job, a 24/7, 365 days a year, including school vacations. Mothers of big families know what I am talking about. A few years later, when the children were a little older, I asked the president of our city's Jewish community, who had already done a lot for us, to find me an office job. He told me that was impossible. So why, some people may ask, did I not start looking for any kind of work that would allow me to earn a little money? Quite simply because I knew that if I started working a job that I disliked, it would not be good either for my children or me. For example, if I had been a maintenance worker for a large compound, I believe—forgive the expression—I would have gone off the rails. The children had already been sufficiently shaken up by their mother's death, and I had to keep my sanity.

Shortly after my wife's death, I told myself that it would be a good idea to move. We needed a change of air. That was how we settled in an inexpensive little house in the southeast suburbs of Paris. By the way, the Jewish community in this suburb was very welcoming and did everything it could to help me; I am very grateful to it. There were only two bedrooms for the six children, but there was a little garden that was very nice. At first, I enrolled the children in the Jewish school. But shortly after I realized that I could no longer afford it despite the discount they were happy to offer. So I enrolled them in the public school right next to our home, which made it a lot more practical and less tiring for me.

During this period, when I was newly a widower, I had a nonpracticing Jewish girlfriend. For a year she was an enormous help. She was the one who suggested sending an email to all the presidents of Jewish communities in order to find housing. She went along with me to visit the little house we moved to. She took the time to move our things in, making multiple roundtrips between the north and south of Paris. She helped me to take care of the children, who liked her a lot. She briefly lived with us and respected the Jewish family rules. But the six children and the constraints of the Law were a lot for her to bear. For my part, I could not become sufficiently attached to her. We decided to break up. Was this relationship kosher, you ask? To tell the truth, no, it was not the kind of thing that is done in the Orthodox Jewish community. But at this period, I was already a little dissident. I felt at peace with my conscience.

For their part, people in the Jewish community were trying to introduce me to women. I met one or two, playing the game for a while, but it did not last. I had built a shell around myself. Something in me did not allow itself to become attached. In fact, I think I had forbidden myself from falling in love. If I became involved in a love affair that did not work, it might deeply affect me. But I could not allow myself to be preoccupied with anything but the children. And at any rate I was not exactly suffering from loneliness.

Paradoxically, during the three years following the death of my wife, now that I was "free" to act any way I wanted, I never went to church and did not wear a cross. I did not purchase the Gospels again, and I no longer meditated. It was not because I felt guilty in relation to my wife; it was just that I did not think about it anymore. However, when I passed in front of a church, I always had the desire to go inside. With hindsight, this latent period showed me that my attraction for Jesus was not sentimental. My relationship with Christ did not come to fill a kind of loneliness. If it did, I would have thrown myself into His arms after losing my wife. No, Christ's love does not fill an affective lack. Besides, my relationship with Jesus was grounded in my childhood and adolescence, periods of my life when I was never deprived of love on the human level.

At the same time, I was distancing myself a little from the Jewish community. My faith and my observance of the Law had not changed, but I did not go to synagogue regularly anymore. I was tired. I was happier staying at home with the children, living according to my own rhythm and not the rhythm of prayers imposed by the synagogue. More and more, I felt the need for a more personal and less formal relationship to God. The way the liturgy at the synagogue was organized did not allow me to dwell in interiority: everything went by very quickly; they were constantly reading and reading some more. When I prayed a psalm, sometimes a word would hit me, and I wanted to pause there in order to meditate on it. That was impossible at the synagogue; you had to keep going! We had no one-on-one time with God. The whole time, everybody prayed together. So, I experienced God at home. I went into my room, I sang, I danced. I prayed according to my own rhythm.

Lustiger Gives Me a Sign on the Beach at Trouville

Of course with only the state welfare we were receiving, we could no longer afford to go on vacation. So sometimes when the weather was good we would all take the train round-trip to Trouville with the 75 percent large-family discount. And it was there on the beach, while I was neither meditating nor contemplating, on Monday, August 6, 2007, three years after my wife's death, that my life started turning upside down. The kids were busy playing at the water's edge. I wandered off a little ways, leaving Rachel, who was thirteen, to watch over her younger siblings. While I was walking on the sand my eyes suddenly caught sight of a large Calvary scene overlooking the beach. And then, as had happened in the past, without my expecting it at all, something very intense took place inside. I felt drawn to Christ again.

I went back toward the children and sat down, a little shaken up by what I had just experienced. I began leafing through a book of Jewish theology while they continued to play around me. Suddenly, in the intense heat, intense chills started running through my body. I had no idea what was happening to me. And I had no idea why I addressed the children at that moment, saying: "Cardinal Lustiger is dying in the hospital!" I had absolutely *no* idea where that came from.

We did not take the train back until eight and got back to the house late. Usually, when we got home, I would give them their baths. But this time I was unsettled and needed to be alone. So I asked the older girls to look after the boys. I urged them not to disturb me and closed myself up in my room. There, I turned on the television and, flipping through the channels, came across the Catholic channel KTO. I was stunned to hear the newscaster announce that Cardinal Lustiger had died the day before! It was a real shock. This was August 6, 2007. On August 6 the Church celebrates the Transfiguration of Christ. The Transfiguration is the extraordinary moment when Jesus led three of his apostles up a mountain and appeared before them transfigured with a stunning whiteness, surrounded by Moses and Elijah (see Mt 17:1–9; Mk 9:2–8; Lk 9:28–36).

This time, the call was clear. Cardinal Lustiger had come to meet me. Jean-Marie Lustiger, a converted Jew, had given me a sign. Christ had worked through him. It was as simple as that. This was the event that would set everything in motion. At the time, I did not explicitly tell myself: "This time, OK, I'm going to convert!" No. I was satisfied with living the experience and following what was happening, without looking ahead to the future. I promised myself that I would see a priest of the Catholic Church in September, when the children were back in school and I would have more time.

I fell asleep with that decision. But as it happened, the Lord beat me to it. In the middle of the night, while I was sleeping peacefully, I was suddenly awakened by the same chills that had come over me on the beach. And then I began to feel the presence of Christ very intensely in my room and even within my body. The experience even went beyond something simply felt. I did not see Him, but I spoke to Him and prostrated myself before Him. If someone had come upon me then, he would certainly have taken me for a total madman.

That was the first but not the last time that this happened to me. Indeed a number of times I was awakened in the middle of the night, around two in the morning, by these chills and this presence. I could not fall back asleep until seven. Since I was not getting enough sleep, I was afraid of being tired and of the smooth functioning of the home suffering for it. But to my great surprise, I felt no more tired than usual. Nothing changed in the course of my daily life, except my relationship with God. During the day, without being lifted up to Heaven, I had incredible experiences. I felt the peace and the intense pleasure of divine love. I had encounters with God, an intimate relationship with Him, that I had never known before. Maybe it was a foretaste of eternal life? Many other people have had this experience of loving rapture, but it cannot be explained with words. It has to be lived to be believed.

With hindsight, I think it is fortunate that I did not see people from the Church at that time. They would probably have been suspicious, and that would have distanced me from them. Indeed it seems to me that some Church officials are too worldly and not daring enough. On the other hand, Benedict XVI, the pope at that time, was diplomatic and prudent but not fearful. I can certainly understand that if I had gone to a priest with my beard and hat to explain that I was drawn to the cross, that Cardinal Lustiger had given me a sign on the beach at Trouville, and that I had mystical chills at night, he would have been perplexed. And of course I am entirely aware that it is necessary to be cautious about this kind of spiritual phenomena. The greatest mystical saints said so again and again. The right approach is to be welcoming and then discerning. But there is a difference between the virtue of prudence, as Saint Thomas Aquinas explains it, and spiritual overcautiousness. Some prelates are afraid of being taken for fools. It seems to me that the Church in France is too self-censuring, out of fear for how she is going to be perceived. It is not at all surprising, then, that some Catholics lack sufficient self-confidence. Moreover, in France a Jew is much more highly regarded and respected than a Catholic. I was soon going to realize this, by experiencing it myself.

John Paul II Gives Me
a Sign on Television

I would like to emphasize what is to my eyes a major point: in our lives the supernatural works through the natural. There is not a space and a time for God on one side, and our lives on the other. There is a connection between the two. Moreover, with the Incarnation, God has taken upon Himself all of human experience. He comes to us through the most trivial intermediaries and through individual persons. This is how He went about it with me.

Not long after, in September 2007, I was watching television with the children, flipping from channel to channel trying to find a good program, when I happened upon a movie about the life of Karol Wojtyla. I have to admit I did not know much about him other than what the news said, and honestly I had never felt any particular interest in Pope John Paul II. Nevertheless, as crazy as it might seem, a scene from this TV movie touched me and spoke to me. When the future John Paul II was young and involved in theater and philosophy, a man gave him a book by Saint John of the Cross. Later, he in turn gave it to one of his Jewish friends. At the exact moment I heard "cross" and "John" I jumped up and told myself: "I have to have that book; I have to get ahold of it!" I immediately planned to buy it as soon as possible. That is how the Lord went about setting me on the path. What would push me to act was not the mystical relationship that I had had with Christ since I was eight (even though as a teenager

I had already made an attempt at conversion that failed because the priest left me alone in the confessional), but merely this TV movie. It was from that precise moment that everything followed, like cascading dominoes. For it is in the tiny events of our ordinary lives that God gives us signs. He truly speaks to us in the details of our daily routines. His transcendence is expressed in our humanity, through our limited reality.

Even so this scene before the television was unbelievable. You have to imagine an Orthodox Jewish family glued to a movie about the pope—and eager to watch the rest on the following days. Watching the movie I began to weep. It was the first time I had cried like that. It was not sorrow, but a form of attraction. When the soul can no longer express what it is experiencing with words, it seeps out through tears. But very quickly I got hold of myself. My reason came to my rescue, saying: "Hey, calm down! You've never read what this pope wrote. He's not your rabbi. Plus, it's not him on the screen but just an actor." Despite all that, I could not deny the emotion that was engulfing me. Heck, why had I started to cry? Why did I have so strong a feeling that this movie was addressed to me, that Someone was speaking to me through it? Oddly, the children were also completely captivated by the movie! They also started to love John Paul II when just the day before they had not even known his name.

From that moment on I started going back to Mass. Each Sunday I would go to a church outside of my neighborhood so as not to be recognized.

Where Are All the Catholics?

As I was saying, from the moment I saw the TV movie about the life of Karol Wojtyla there was only one idea in my head: to get a copy of the book by Saint John of the Cross that Karol Wojtyla had given to his Jewish friend. So where could I find one? I decided to go first to the big bookstore FNAC. But, unlike what you might think, getting there was no easy feat. Once more, mothers will know what I am talking about! The first obstacle I had to face was finding the time to go there since everything in my day was timed by stopwatch. One afternoon I started off. I dashed to the Saint-Lazare FNAC, which was at the end of my metro line. It was the start of a race against the clock since I knew I absolutely had to be back before the children came home from school. Coming out of the metro station, I ran all the way to the FNAC and up the stairs four steps at a time to the book department. I rushed over to the religion section. I was completely out of breath. I looked for the book by Saint John of the Cross but did not see it. I hurried over to ask a salesman. He suggested I go to La Procure. I told him that I was not familiar with that bookstore. He responded by staring at me in disbelief. He seemed amazed that a man who wanted to read Saint John of the Cross had never heard of La Procure! So I made up a story, stammering that I was not from Paris. He gave me the address and the metro stop nearest to it. But it was already too late for me to make it there. So I went home with the address in my pocket.

A few days later, I could finally make it to La Procure. Going inside the bookstore, I had the strange feeling of having been there before. Yet that was hardly likely. Not wanting to waste time, I went directly to a saleswoman and asked her if she had books by Saint John of the Cross. She looked at me, surprised, as if it was obvious. I was relieved and very impatient too. I asked her where to find them, and she answered, "In the Saints section." That did not mean much to me, so she brought me over to it. I took a book at random from the shelf. It was *The Living Flame of Love*, a book consisting of a poem that he had written for a laywoman. It was his last work, which summed up all the others. I opened it on the spot and glanced through it. Suddenly I had something like a flashback, a spark: I remembered a dream I had had a few days before in which I saw myself in a bookstore reading Saint John of the Cross. Well, there I was in those surroundings to the last detail. I had the strong feeling I was living in a fantasy film.

I decided to buy not one, not two, but all of the books by Saint John of the Cross in paperback as well as the Gospels. I had not opened the Gospels since throwing them out under my wife's injunction after the burglary more than ten years earlier. Leaving the bookstore, I told myself that I could not keep to myself anymore, that I had to find someone I could talk to about everything. This time I had to go all the way. But how should I go about it? Whom should I go find?

Are you wondering why I did not go to see a priest in a church? Obviously I had thought of that, but it was easier said than done—especially after that failed meeting at Sacré-Cœur when I was a teenager that had left me with such a bad memory. The priest, rather than taking me by the hand and saying "Come, my son, I am going to introduce you to someone", had left me alone! This kind of bad experience can have a lasting effect and act as a barrier to a reunion with Christ.

For that reason I wanted to meet a Catholic outside the context of a church. However I did not know how to do that. For no one in the Catholic Church had ever come toward me. Jehovah's Witnesses, sure; I remembered them! But no Catholic had ever come up to me in the street. Nor had I ever received letters from the pastor in my mailbox. Certainly, there are new communities in the Catholic Church that are very active in evangelization—that is, in proclaiming the faith and reaching out to people. But they are a drop of water in an ocean. At that moment I asked myself the question, where are all the Catholics? When you are looking for them, you have no idea where to find them. It seems of great necessity to me that Christians bear witness by wearing a sign that allows them to be recognized. Indeed, why should only priests and religious be distinctively marked? Why are there so few lay Catholics who wear a cross around the neck or a Virgin Mary medal? By wanting to fit in with the world too much, we let ourselves be gobbled up by the secular spirit. We must not be afraid! John Paul II said as much: "Be not afraid!" And as Jesus says in the Gospel of John: "If the world hates you, know that it has hated me before it hated you" (15:18). Of course, it is not a question of being provocative or offensive, but of being personally coherent. How can I bear witness to Christ through my actions if the people around me do not know that I am a Christian?

So I decided to go back to La Procure to find Catholics. But I was so much in my Jewish bubble that to my mind, as I was just saying, a Catholic would have to be wearing a distinctive sign, like an Orthodox Jew. So I did not find any. Then I went to see another saleswoman, at random. I asked her if she knew any Catholics who follow Saint John of the Cross, the way a Jew follows a rabbi.

"You're looking for Carmelites."

I said yes, not knowing what she was talking about.

"You're in luck!"

"Why?"

"I'm a secular Carmelite!"

"What is that?"

She seemed surprised, but she explained. Members of a Third Order are laypersons attached to a religious order. She then asked me if I wanted to meet with a priest and gave me the telephone number of Father Y. It was unbelievable! I could not get over it: on the first try I happened on a Third Order Carmelite, admittedly in a religious bookstore, but not all the salespeople at La Procure are necessarily Christian, much less close to the spirituality of Saint John of the Cross.

I really felt Someone was leading me. This is the charismatic life, and it is not reserved to a community or a current in the Church called Charismatic. The charismatic life consists in letting yourself act and be guided by the Holy Spirit in everyday life, in all circumstances. It is like being on a sailboat: you move along when you hoist the sails for the wind of the Spirit to breathe upon. If not, you stagnate, and you miss the people and the signs He places on your path to direct you. Each Christian is called to experience the promptings of the Holy Spirit in his family, work, and social life, and not only in moments allocated to prayer. The spiritual life is one with the natural life, even if it is essential to have times dedicated to mental or other forms of prayer.

Every morning from that day on, I have read Saint John of the Cross at breakfast. I really appreciate what he wrote because it is founded on the Word lived and experienced. I read him even when I do not feel like it, out of fidelity, for he is my big brother.

Attempts at Jewish-Christian Dialogue

I let a few days pass. Then I finally decided to call Father Y. I introduced myself, explaining that a saleswoman at La Procure had given me his number and that I was Jewish and interested in Christ. He listened to me and suggested I meet him at his home near Porte d'Auteuil.

Throughout the fall I visited him regularly. During these meetings we talked a lot about Saint John of the Cross. What I experienced then is to my mind real Jewish-Christian dialogue. Each person is faithful to himself; neither one denies who he is. He explained Saint John of the Cross from the perspective of his theological formation. And I explained how I understood him coming from my Jewish philosophical and mystical culture. Father Y. welcomed everything I had to say. He never came across as peremptory or arrogant. He did not say: "You'll understand someday!" For that matter, I did not feel he was trying to influence me in any way. In the course of our discussions, I realized that words do not always have the same meaning in every culture. Consequently mutual understanding is impossible so long as you have not first settled on the meaning of words. For example, the word "flesh" for Saint Paul or for a Jew does not have the same meaning as for a Greek.

Father Y.'s humility was truly exceptional. When someone is rooted in God and in the Church, he is not afraid to listen to different opinions; he can let himself be enriched by new points of view without losing his grounding in what is essential. I have already said earlier what I think about interreligious dialogue when it is not founded on truth. What I experienced with Father Y. proves to me that a rich theological dialogue between Jews and Christians is possible. Moreover, there are other examples, like that of Saint Bernard of Clairvaux, who went to study with the rabbis at Troyes. He opposed the pogroms and wanted to see for himself how the Jewish exegetes whom he found so interesting went about their studies. But he was not afraid to say that truth was within the Church. Another example: in his *Discussions about the Our Father*, Cardinal Journet uses a concept from Jewish mystical theology, the phenomenon of God's contraction at the moment of Creation. Saint John of the Cross also maintained dialogue with a contemporary Jewish Spanish mystical theologian.

My encounters with the Church and my attempts at dialogue with her representatives were not always so fruitful. Indeed, later, I often met priests who did not have Father Y.'s capacity for listening and who tried to impose their point of view on me. My Christian reading of the Old Testament scared them because they imagined it harmed Jewish-Christian dialogue or the Church's Magisterium and Tradition. In France, where there is a common tendency to believe that there is nothing new to be learned, many priests make an idol of their intelligence. They speak through French culture and their own formation, both influenced by the Enlightenment and by Descartes. I like to be able to debate with theologians about probing questions concerning the explanation of the Faith or the Scriptures. However I must say that I am often confronted by a lack of openness in this area that is hard to bear. Moreover I encounter the same phenomenon among religious sisters and the laity. The attitude of some priests

might have turned me against the Church, but I understood that they were men and that like everybody they
have their personalities, childhood wounds, and faults. A
priest is a human being like you and me. He is not pure
spirit. Of course, by virtue of the sacrament of holy orders,
which makes him act *in persona Christi* at the moment of
the Consecration, he has a responsibility that surpasses him
since another Person is involved. However, it would be
too easy to throw stones at the whole Church because
some priests or bishops act badly, or not as one would
hope. For indeed there are also great priests and bishops!

After my baptism, when I was beginning to teach, I would
meet priests and bishops with whom I would have real
intellectual and spiritual exchanges. For a year immediately after my baptism, I would meet with Father Thibault,
a Brother of Saint John the Theologian, with whom I
would discuss the thought of Saint Thomas Aquinas. My
bishop, the Most Reverend Michel Santier, who is a true
father to me, has for several years given me free formation
in theology and commissioned me in my contemporary
apostolate within the Catholic Church for the entire public
in France and abroad. My tutor is the dean of theology
for the Brothers of Saint John. We have rich and wide-
ranging discussions. I also meet regularly with the Most
Reverend Michel Aupetit, an auxiliary bishop of Paris, for
enjoyable talks. He has invited me to give lectures to the
priests of Paris as part of their continuing formation.

Today, commissioned by Bishop Santier to give conferences and preach retreats in France and abroad, I have
the opportunity to discover the Church's full palette, in
her variety and riches, with her shortfalls and her beauty.
At first, since some people had closed the door on me,
especially after my baptism, I felt the Church was not
welcoming. Now, my perspective has changed. I have

learned to love the Church, or rather Jesus has taught me to love her as He loves her: unto death! When He died on the Cross, He was acutely aware that the Church, the community of first Christians, was not perfect. And this is to be expected because the Church is made up of her members, of individuals. Thus one dimension of the Church is divine and holy since she is founded in Jesus, and the other dimension is sinful. The same conflict plays out on the anthropological level between the new man, the child of God who does not sin, and the old man who corresponds to our fallen humanity. It is important to remember that the Church is founded on Peter, the same Peter who denied Jesus three times on the night of His trial, who was not present when He was crucified, and who did not believe Mary Magdalene when, on the morning of the Resurrection, she went to Peter to proclaim that she had seen Jesus. And yet, after all that, Jesus did not say to Peter: "Since you were not up to it, I am firing you; you are no longer worthy to be the rock on which I desire to found my Church!" Rather, He asked him three times: "[D]o you love me?" (see Jn 21:15–17). And each time, Jesus asked Peter to feed His sheep.

I would also note that throughout the centuries in His marriage of love with the Church, and despite all her infidelities, Christ has never divorced her. So, yes, it is painful to meet priests who close the door of their churches on us. But the Church is beautiful and holy in her union with Christ, and indispensable for giving us Jesus. It is amazing, but little by little I began to see and experience the Church as the Bride of Christ and our mother who gives us birth in God.

Let us get back to Father Y. In the course of our discussions, he explained to me that the Gospels are the complete accomplishment of the Scriptures. So, I questioned him:

"Where we do we see in the Old Testament that the Messiah will be born of a young virgin?"

"Isaiah 7:14."

"That doesn't work!" I told him.

He looked at me, perplexed.

"Why doesn't that work?"

"Because what's written there is 'alma', which means 'young woman'. This word that gets translated 'virgin' designated all unmarried women. 'A virgin shall give birth' in biblical language simply means 'a woman is going to give birth', neither more nor less. It does not mean a virgin birth. Plus, in order for it to correspond with the prophecy of Isaiah, at the Annunciation in the Gospel of Saint Luke, the angel Gabriel should have called Mary's child Emmanuel."

I was totally disarmed by Father Y.'s magnificent, Christlike humility. Indeed, he never tried to convince me. He responded that Mary's virginity is a question of faith. But there was nothing to be done; I was *not* convinced. Moreover, I was closed-minded about all questions concerning the Virgin Mary, and Father Y. would quickly come to realize that. On that particular day, he did not persist. However, the question of the Virgin Mary came up again very soon. Another day, he started talking about her. I responded:

"I'm not interested in the Virgin Mary!"

He looked at me inquisitively.

"Nope, not interested."

"Why?"

He was trying to understand my reluctance. Somebody else might have said, "But you have to be interested! The Virgin Mary is an intermediary!" But not him. He went on: "Why do you say that praying to the Virgin Mary is idolatry?"

"When I turn on KTO and see all these processions at Lourdes, these candles and prostrations before statues, it's like idols in Asia, Africa, or the Bible."

He did not respond and we went back to our reading of Saint John of the Cross. Once more, he was not trying to persuade me of anything.

I Fall in Love with Mary

During this period when I was regularly meeting with Father Y., I was still being awakened at night by chills to find myself in the presence of Jesus. I had never spoken to anyone about this, but I decided to confide in my new friend. The day I did, he listened to me but did not respond in any special way. We went on talking about Saint John of the Cross. The next time, though, he asked me a number of questions about what was happening to me during the night. I felt like I was being submitted to a real investigation. At the time I wished I had kept silent. He wanted to know everything: the hour it came on, what my state of consciousness was at that time, how I felt afterward during the day, whether an interior voice was speaking to me, etc. At least he took it seriously, I told myself.

Another day he asked if I was still being awakened up at night. I responded in the affirmative. He then suggested I say the Rosary the next time I started to feel these chills. I responded: "That sounds fine, but what's the Rosary?"

"It's a set of meditations."

"OK, I'm familiar with that; Jews meditate too! Tell me about it."

"It's made up of saying one Our Father and ten Hail Marys."

"Oh no! I already told you: I'm not interested in Mary!"

So I proposed a compromise: "If you want, I can say eleven Our Fathers instead of the ten Hail Marys!"

He smiled and said: "No, it doesn't work that way! I have another suggestion to make: say 'Hail Mary' as if you were saying good morning to her—no statue, no getting on your knees."

Then he handed me a leaflet of John Paul II's meditations on the five luminous mysteries and explained how I should pray one mystery for each decade of the Rosary. I said to myself: "Look, John Paul II again!" I saw it as a sign, so I accepted. While I was leaving, Father Y. asked me to call and tell him what happened. Later I would understand that he wanted to verify that these nocturnal phenomena were not from the devil, because Mary drives back the devil.

Leaving his place that evening, I was very worked up and wondered how I was going to manage to wait until night. The evening with the children seemed endless. I was waiting for one thing only: for them to go to bed so that I could be alone and look over the leaflet. Finally the moment arrived when I could retire to my room. I then began, with the help of a rosary and the flier, so that I would know what I was doing when I was awakened. I was nervous, as if I were preparing to take a test. So I recited four sets of mysteries—joyful, luminous, sorrowful, and glorious—before going to bed. Then I fell fast asleep and slumbered like a baby—until morning! As it happened, since that Rosary, I have not been awakened at night! Instead, when I opened my eyes in the morning, I was filled with a crazy desire to prostrate myself at Mary's feet, to show her my love. Unbelievable, no? Jesus led me to Mary, His Mother, while usually it is the reverse: one comes to Jesus through Mary.

More and more, I was torn up inside between what I was experiencing in my heart and what my reason was telling me. I was fed up with it. To find a solution to this interior dilemma, I decided to grant my heart three months to have its experiences and to put aside my reason during that time. At the end of those three months, I would draw my conclusions. To begin with, I went back to La Procure. Walking through the aisles, a book drew my attention. It was *True Devotion to Mary* by Saint Louis-Marie Grignion de Montfort. The author was a complete stranger to me. I bought the book and started reading it immediately. That book showed me that just as God passed through Mary to join man, He desires that we in our turn pass through Mary to join Him. What mysterious delicacy!

One evening not long after, when I could not fall asleep, I received something like an interior word. This word explained to me why Mary had to be a virgin to receive the Messiah, and it did so through the means of Jewish mystical theology! According to tradition, Sarah, Abraham's wife, was barren because it was necessary to break the natural line of procreation from the sin of Eve in order for her to give birth to a pure nation. A kind of death and rebirth was necessary. For Isaac to be pure, his receptacle had to be pure. This notion of appropriate measure between the receptacle and what it contains is fundamental in Jewish mystical theology. Water goes in a glass and not in a flat plate! This same idea can be found in the second chapter of Exodus. That chapter says that a man "took to wife a daughter of Levi" and that Moses was born of their union. And yet we know that this young woman already had two children, Miriam and Aaron. So why do the Scriptures speak of her as if she were a virgin? The Talmud explains: God worked a miracle in restoring virginity to the mother of Moses because it was necessary that the savior of Israel be born of a virgin mother. This revelation had such an impact on me that at that moment Mary entered completely into my heart.

The Sisters of Bethlehem

By November 2007, several months had passed since the day Jean-Marie Lustiger had given me a sign on the beach at Trouville. For some time I had made a habit of walking around Saint Augustine Church in the afternoons while the children were in school. Saint Augustine's is a very big, circular church with a number of chapels. In one of these, the one where Charles de Foucauld was converted, there is a truly magnificent crucifix. It was there I would sit down, always in the same spot, facing Him. At the time, I was unfamiliar with Charles de Foucauld and did not go there because of him; but with hindsight, I feel the place of his conversion was important and, who knows, maybe he played a role in Heaven in my own conversion?

One day when I came into the chapel I noticed a nun seated in "my" chair. Since I was beginning to believe that there are no coincidences, I decided to speak to her. We talked briefly. She explained that she was a Little Sister of Bethlehem and came from Fontainebleau. The Little Sisters of Bethlehem are cloistered contemplatives who, in principle, never leave their monastery. Never? So what was she doing there that day, in my chair, at the very moment I came into the church? Putting me on the path to the Church, that much is certain! She suggested I go to the priory of the Sisters of Bethlehem at Place Victor-Hugo in Paris.

So very shortly after, I went to the address she had given me. I entered through the shop, on the side, and asked if I could meet a sister. I was then introduced to Sister C., to whom I related my story and my attraction to Jesus. She listened to me and then told me I absolutely had to meet a certain Sister P., which I did. The first time, we had a nice exchange in the parlor. She suggested I come back to see her when I felt like it. I did not need to be persuaded: I came back as often as I could. That was how hours and hours of discussion started.

In December 2007, Sister P. invited me to spend Christmas in the monastery. What a joy! I had dreamed of this so much since my childhood; I was *finally* going to celebrate Christmas in a church. Obviously, I immediately accepted her invitation. She suggested staying over and promised I could eat kosher. Anyway, that would not be too difficult for the sisters because there were all sorts of Jewish shops in one of the streets neighboring the monastery. Coming home that day, I was full of emotion. I could *not* believe it. A song by Enrico Macias, "Christmas in Jerusalem", was stuck in my head. Whereas for me, it would be, "Christmas in Bethlehem"! D-day arrived. I waited for the children to fall asleep before slipping away. They were under Rachel's supervision; I had left her my telephone number just in case. I had not told them where I was going. It was hard leaving them alone for the night; it was the first time it had happened. But I felt that I had to go to the monastery. On the way, I prayed that nothing would happen to them.

The Mass was magnificent. I received the Body and Blood of Christ. Sister P. did not mention it, and when I later admitted to her that I had first received Communion at thirteen, she was stupefied. Then, like the sisters, I took my meal in a cell. Finally, I went to sleep. Sleeping in the monastery was a very moving experience for me. The incredible silence there made a deep impression on me. It was an experience of great contemplation and relief. I felt totally cut off from the world. I tasted an interior peace and joy that I had never known anywhere else.

When I left the monastery the next morning, the sisters gave me some bread and cakes for the children. When I got home, I distributed these little presents, explaining that they came from a monastery where I had spent the night. To my great surprise, the children made no comment. Sister P. had also given me a crucifix and a statue of Our Lady of Lourdes that she had me pick out in their gift shop. I did not intend to show those gifts to the children for the time being. I carefully hid them in my room. For despite everything that had happened to me in those last months, the children still had no idea what was going on, and we continued to lead our normal ultra-Orthodox Jewish life.

However, the more it went on the more I felt that, this time, I was not going to give it up. Conversion was close—I was going to go through to the other side. For this reason I was beginning seriously to ask myself how I was going to explain things to the children. How would they take it? I was very apprehensive about their reaction. So I tried to lay the ground little by little. For example, whereas since Christmas the statue of Mary had been hidden in a drawer in my room, and I had always closed the door before praying to her, I decided to make the statue more visible and leave the door ajar. One day I practically left the door open. Rebecca came in and caught me on my knees before the Virgin Mary. She asked me what I was doing. A Jew prays seated or standing, but not on his knees. I was a little anxious but at the same time, I had looked forward to this moment. I explained to her:

"She's the Virgin Mary, the Mother of Jesus."

"Is she your new girlfriend?" she asked.

That was it; I had been worried for nothing. From then on, the Virgin Mary was accepted in our home. Whenever we lit the Shabbat candles on Friday evenings from that day on, we also sang the Hail Mary.

Sister P. had also invited me to spend New Year's at the monastery. This time I let the children know beforehand. That evening also began with prayer. The Little Sisters of Bethlehem are very Marian, and there were numerous hymns addressed to the Virgin Mary because January 1 is one of her feast days. Honoring the Mother of Jesus, who had only very recently become part of my life, held a very special significance for me. The following morning they again gave me cakes for the children, who asked me how things had gone when I got home. I told them about my Christian New Year's.

I was amazed at how they reacted. They took things in stride, without getting worked up. You surely think that I was fortunate and that my children were very relaxed and open-minded. But I do not believe in luck; I believe in Providence, formation, and the trusting relationship between parents and children that can develop within a family. A few months later, before going to the Holy Land, I would ask my daughters to cover my book by Saint John of the Cross with opaque paper so that I would not be recognized as an apostate Jew. Then Déborah responded: "Do whatever you want, Dad!" They were more open-minded than I was. I listened to her and did not cover up my book, and sure enough a Jewish woman on the bus questioned me.

More and more I dreamed about baptism, but I was torn up inside. On February 2, 2008, for the feast of the Presentation of Jesus in the Temple, I returned to the monastery. I went to Evening Prayer, spent the night in a cell, and then attended Mass early in the morning. Before leaving again, around three o'clock, Sister P. asked me how I was doing, "Great!" I replied. "By the way, I've decided to ask to be baptized!" I was surprised myself by what I had just said. At that exact moment, God knows why, my interior conflict had ended. Sister P. asked me why I wanted to be baptized, and I said I wanted to be a Christian! She then explained that I would have to enter the catechumenate.

"What's that?"

"It's a preparation for baptism."

"Excuse me, but what am I going to be prepared for?"

"To be a Christian!"

"But I'm ready now! I know how to read the Bible! Anyway, this preparation for baptism you're suggesting is against the Scriptures!"

"Oh really, how so?"

"In the Acts of the Apostles, when the Ethiopian asks Philip for baptism, he bends over a pool of water and baptizes him right away! And Saint Paul, was he asked to enroll in the catechumenate?"

"Calm down!"

"I am calm."

"The Church, it's not like that anymore—"

"But I'm talking to you about Jesus, not about the Church! We're not on the same wavelength!"

Then we had a long discussion in which Sister P. tried to explain to me that the Church and Jesus make up one single body.

A Full-Time Catechumen

For me as a religious Jew my absolute reference point was God's Word, not men's ideas. So what bothered me about the catechumenate was that the Acts of the Apostles never mentions it. Notice how hard it was for the apostle Peter to let go of what was commanded in the Torah. Even so, he said that Jesus was the Messiah, saw the resurrected Jesus, believed and affirmed that Jesus was God and man, received the Holy Spirit at Pentecost, and went off to preach! But despite all of this, he was still convinced that eating kosher was required for the simple and sensible reason that it was written down in the Bible. He would need a vision in order to understand that it was no longer necessary (see Acts 10:9–16).

As far as I was concerned, it was through obedience and because my desire for baptism was stronger than my skepticism about the catechumenate that I agreed to submit to Sister P.'s request. In February 2008 I entered the catechumenate. Some had suggested I approach the Messianic Jews (Jews who believe that Jesus is the Messiah) instead of the Catholic Church, which would probably have been easier for me. However, I was drawn to Catholicism. I did not know why, but there was no doubt in my mind about that, at least. Moreover, some Messianic Jews do not believe in the Trinity, so becoming a Messianic Jew would not have resolved my conflict of conscience, which was chiefly attached to the Person of Jesus, God made man, and to the idea of one God in three Persons.

When talking about Jews like himself who had become Christians, Cardinal Lustiger spoke of fulfilled Jews. I am not trying to shock anyone, but I do not agree with him. I do not consider myself a fulfilled Jew, but rather a Jew converted to Christ. There is no discussion of fulfilled Jews in the Acts of the Apostles or in the Epistles of Saint Paul or anywhere in the Holy Bible. The people who listened to Saint Peter, the head of the Church, asked him and the apostles: "Brethren, what shall we do?" Peter answered: "Repent, and be baptized" (Acts 2:37–38), which led to their conversion. He did not ask them to become fulfilled Jews by welcoming Jesus. A conversion is a total change of direction. Suddenly, you see, think, and eat differently. You have a different relationship with others and with God. After their conversions, Saint Paul, Rabbi Drach, the Libermanns, and Chief Rabbi Zolli of Rome, who had all been Orthodox Jews, saw the practice of the Law differently.

Conversion, *teshuva* in Hebrew, is a return to God. Indeed, in the Holy Scriptures God often asks the straying Jews to be converted, that is, to return to Him. Saint Peter asked the Jews to convert because he believed the Jewish people were straying by not accepting Jesus as God the Savior. In converting to Christ, I became a different person. In my opinion, most nonbelieving or nonpracticing Jews who have converted to Christianity always wind up finding their Jewish roots through Catholicism. It seems to me that they are often uneasy with a Jewish identity that they did not fully accept or live out. They have an outsider's view of Judaism—that is, of Orthodox Judaism and the practice and study of the Law. Chief Rabbi Zolli, who converted in 1945—after a long acquaintanceship with Pope Pius XII, from whom he took his baptismal name, Eugenio—had no sense of infidelity to his roots because he had fully lived and fulfilled his Judaism. Saint Paul, too, did not find it hard to give up his Jewish practices. Nor did Saint John spend hours talking about his Judaism.

On the subject of Cardinal Lustiger, I would like to open a parenthesis. When John Paul II proposed naming him archbishop of Paris, his Vatican entourage was opposed, thinking that the fact he was Jewish would make waves. John Paul II did not back down. He went off to pray. When he came back, he told his counselors: it is the will of God, period. All his life Cardinal Lustiger suffered because Jews did not recognize Jesus and because many in the Church did not recognize that Jesus was a Jew. One more thing: Cardinal Lustiger did not convert out of convenience. He was baptized in the middle of the Second World War against the wishes of his parents, who relented because they thought it would protect him. His mother died in a concentration camp, and his father asked him to call off his baptism—how torn up he must have felt! I can easily imagine the state of his conscience and how he must have felt he was betraying his family. It seems to me only converted Jews and Muslims can truly understand what Jesus means when He declares in the Gospel of Matthew: "Do not think that I have come to bring peace on earth; I have not come to bring peace, but a sword. For I have come to set a man against his father, and a daughter against her mother, and a daughter-in-law against her mother-in-law" (10:34–35).

Let me get back to my catechumenate. This long period of preparation for baptism that was just starting looked like an obstacle course to me. And believe me, this is the case for a great many catechumens. I sincerely think that this time of preparation (which in France sometimes lasts two or three years) should be abbreviated as soon as a real desire for baptism has been discerned in the catechumen.

Besides, it would be much wiser for the Catholic Church to follow the neophyte *after* his baptism rather than *before*. Indeed after baptism, the new Christian often finds himself completely left to his own devices. No one seems seriously interested in him, and thus sometimes the newly baptized Christian never again sets foot in a church.

A layperson from the Bethlehem community, François F., was entrusted with being my sponsor. This task that fell to him was far from easy. After all I was coming to him with ten years of rabbinical training behind me and a whole theology and philosophy. I was not a pagan who had just converted. He could not answer all my questions. He even admitted to me that he was out of his league, and I could easily understand that. At the same time, I was also being watched over by a priest, Father O. Here too, our dialogue was difficult, as much for him as for *me*. I did not stop asking him questions, and I was not convinced by the answers he gave me. I always had an argument to use against him. But he showed himself to be rather closed to dialogue. He wanted to impose his point of view on me: he was the priest and a "specialist" in Saint Paul, as he put it. Given my cultural customs, Father O.'s way of doing things really shocked me. Remember that in Judaism, the custom is to dispute, in the medieval sense, as I practiced it at the yeshiva. *Disputatio* is a part of one's studies, just as Saint Thomas Aquinas in his time defended his theological points of view. In the yeshiva, you can disagree with the teacher. On the other hand, the way classes of Catholic theology and exegesis are organized, usually in a lecture hall, no one would *ever* think of contradicting the professor. This is a shame because the practice of *disputatio* allows you to see an argument through to the end and to clarify things. For no one here below has a full grasp of the truth. No word of ours will exhaust the mystery: "God has said but one Word, and this is his Son" (Saint John of the Cross). Several points of view can participate in shedding light on this mystery from different angles. Moreover, in his Rule, Saint Benedict insists on the fact that the Holy Spirit often speaks through the littlest of all the brothers in a community, the one no one would think to ask.

Throughout my entire catechumenate, I butted heads with the way the sayings of Jesus were presented to me. The fact that Jesus was a Jew was completely obscured. Obviously I am not saying you have to be a Jew to understand Jesus. The Fathers of the Church and the saints who were not Jewish passed down the Gospels just fine, and Jesus Himself said: "I thank you, Father, ... that you have hidden these things from the wise and understanding and revealed them to infants" (Mt 11:25; Lk 10:21). Nevertheless, I think that in order to enter fully into the words of Jesus, you first need to enter into Jewish thought, for Jesus addressed Jews, with whom He shared the same Jewish culture. The context of the rabbinic culture of the era is also very important. For my part, when I undertook formation in theology and philosophy a few years later and was going to study the thought of Saint Thomas Aquinas, I needed to understand who he was and where and when he lived in order to enter into his language and his culture. Even after years of study, I would admit that that is not my culture. This seems like an essential step to me. Anyway, things are going in this direction since the Second Vatican Council and recent Jewish-Christian dialogue.

When Father O. quoted this saying of Christ in the Gospel of Matthew: "I have come not to abolish them [the law and the prophets] but to fulfil them" (5:17), I did not understand it. For me, that was false. We should not forget that Jesus was addressing Jewish Pharisees here. For them the Law meant the sum of Moses' proscriptions gathered in the five books that comprise the Pentateuch, the Torah. Yet, Christ certainly came to abolish these Jewish rituals and notably eating kosher, when He said: "[N]ot what goes into the mouth defiles a man, but what comes out of the mouth, this defiles a man" (Mt 15:11). And eating kosher was not invented by Moses or a few rabbis; it was a commandment given by God to Moses. It was *no* small thing. If tomorrow someone came with the best intentions in the world to abolish the Eucharist, what would we say? So I pestered Father O. with my questions: "What did Christ mean? What word did He use in Aramaic? How did Saint Jerome, working from the Septuagint and the Hebrew Bibles, translate these verbs 'abolish' and 'fulfill'?"

Furthermore, it must be understood that Jesus did not come only to abolish Jewish rituals but also to abolish the dogmas of Jewish faith. Indeed, the prophets had never led us to believe in a Trinitarian God who would become flesh. So that was another point on which I sharply interrogated Father O.: "Where do we see proclamations of the Trinitarian God—Father, Son, and Holy Spirit—in the Old Testament?" I was not convinced by what he showed me. For example, the prophecy of Isaiah about the birth of the Messiah (7:14) could be referring to a merely human leader. Even though many Christian translations of the Bible use the word "virgin" the original Hebrew does not say that the woman in question is going to conceive virginally. Also, the text does not explicitly state that God is going to become flesh. To my Jewish eyes, the Trinity abolished the number one commandment of Judaism: "Hear, O Israel: The LORD our God is one" (Deut 6:4). For a Jew, a triune God is incompatible with the One God. Here too, Father O. showed a lack of openness. He did not take my point of view into consideration. He did not understand that with human reason alone, no one in the world could see that there is a Trinitarian God or a God who becomes incarnate. In the Gospel of Matthew Christ asks His disciples: "But who do you say that I am?" Saint Peter, the foundation of the Church, answers Him: "You are the Christ, the Son of the living God." Then Jesus makes this declaration: "Blessed are you, Simon Bar-Jona! For flesh and blood has not revealed this to you, but my Father who is in heaven" (16:15–17). Thus, what Peter said, he did not understand through his own intelligence; it was revealed to him from on high. Likewise, Saul would need to be illuminated in order to understand these things.

Later, after I was illuminated and had been baptized and received the Holy Spirit, I would understand this saying of Jesus differently: "I have come not to abolish them [the law and the prophets] but to fulfil them" (Mt 5:17). Jesus was speaking about the essence of the Old Testament revelation, and this essence is that the Word became flesh. All the Scriptures say only that. All of the Old Testament, all of the Law, is there to announce the Incarnation of the Word that is accomplished in Jesus. All the Scriptures have as their project the bringing forth of the Messiah. Take one example that reveals God's intrinsic project for Abraham. A midrash asks why Abraham takes his nephew Lot with him when he goes into the Promised Land. The midrash's answer is that the Holy Spirit showed Abraham in a vision that the Messiah would come forth from the descendants of Lot.* There we have it: Jesus did not come to abolish God's project but to fulfill it, that is, realize it, make it real. Jesus did not come to abolish the Law

---

* Lot's eldest daughter gives birth to Moab, from whom Ruth, the Moabite, is a descendant. Ruth, in turn, becomes the grandmother of King David, from whom the Messiah will be descended.

and the prophets insofar as their aim was the Incarnation of the Word of God. He did not abolish God's intention, which is to redeem man and to reconcile with him in order for him to become truly a child of God: He fulfilled it. How does the Old Testament prepare for the New Testament? Not at the level of the prophecies, because in the Creed, we do not say: "I believe in the prophecies!" So how does the Old Testament prepare for the Creed, which is the whole of the Christian life? How do we see the Trinity and the God who is going to become flesh, in the Old Testament?

Meanwhile, I could not take seriously the correspondences between the Old and New Testaments that Father O. was trying to show me. John the Baptist designated Jesus as the "Lamb of God, who takes away the sin of the world" (Jn 1:29), but the lamb offered in the Temple at Passover was a memorial lamb, not an expiatory one. It is on Yom Kippur that the expiatory sacrifice takes place, and it is a goat, *not* a lamb, that is sacrificed. From this I concluded, contrary to what Father O. kept repeating, that Jesus broke the Old Covenant and that there was *no* continuity.

How hard it is for a Jew to adhere to the words of Christ. We see in the Gospels that when Jesus proclaims something that exceeds human reason, people leave Him. Thus in the Gospel of Saint John, many disciples go away when Jesus says: "[H]e who eats my flesh and drinks my blood has eternal life" (6:54). And yet, they had chosen to follow Him; they had given up the material and spiritual security they had known before for Him. But what Jesus says here is above everything; it completely surpasses human reason—eating a man's flesh and drinking his blood?! Besides, once again, where is it written in the Old Testament that the Jews must eat the flesh and drink the blood of a human being, of God incarnate? We cannot incriminate these people who left Jesus at that moment. It has to be realized that Christianity is founded on folly— the folly of the Cross. In other words, the foundation of Christianity is beyond human reason, beyond human perception. The Jews cannot be reproached for not seeing that Jesus was God, for who can see that? It is grasped through faith and through the grace of God.

My Heart and My Head

Sister P. gave me a real talking to! After having bent over backward for me, she was afraid I was going to ruin everything. In short, because of my attitude, Father O. thought that I did not really desire baptism. And yet that was *not* true. So I made a firm decision to stop asking the priest questions. But that did not keep me from asking them to myself. It was still the same exhausting conflict: my heart longed for baptism but my head would not accept it.

One sleepless night I made a deal with Jesus. I spoke to Him with an open heart: "You've placed a desire in my heart, but my head doesn't believe anything about You! It thinks You're a blasphemer, a liar, that You turned the Jewish people away from the true faith! I don't believe in the Trinitarian God or in the Resurrection. If You were resurrected, it's the work of the devil; it's a test God is giving us! It's clearly written in Deuteronomy that if God sends a false prophet, he does so to test us (see Deut 13:1–5). You are God's prophecy! I went to see Your Church: they have no answer to give me. So it's simple: either You set something off in my head, as You did with the chief rabbi of Rome—one day, he opened the Ark and saw Jesus blessing him and telling him 'I no longer need you here, I need you elsewhere'—or You strike me down like Saint Paul, or else You leave me alone, because it's already hard enough as it is raising six children! I don't want to go crazy, I can't allow myself to become unhinged, I have to meet my family's needs! The children have already suffered a shock with the death of their mom; I don't want them to suffer a second shock because their father converts to Catholicism. So do something for the children, too. Or else leave me in peace! Amen." No answer.

A little while later, Sister P. invited me to spend Pentecost at the monastery with the whole family. We had already spent three days there at Easter, all seven of us. Just imagine an observant Jewish family with six children spending three days in a contemplative monastery in the middle of Paris—following the whole Catholic liturgy and eating kosher! It was no small thing for the sisters either. I was a little afraid of how the children would react, especially the girls. They had never been in a monastery before; they might have grumbled about it. But everything went very well. The children enjoyed it, especially the girls who were able to chat with the sisters. I was surprised by how easily they adapted. For that matter, since starting to sing prayers to Mary at the opening of Shabbat, the children had never been opposed to my suggestions. That alone was a miracle, since the oldest girls were already becoming teenagers and *never* at a loss for words. Nevertheless, this time I turned down Sister P.'s invitation because I was afraid the boys would go stir-crazy. So Sister P. suggested I go stay with other Sisters of Bethlehem located in Nemours: they had a garden and the boys would be able to play outside.

So all seven of us arrived on Thursday evening. Friday morning, at last, Jesus was going to reveal himself to me concretely. In one instant, all my questions were going to find their answers. I was going to plunge into another dimension.

The Coup de Grâce

Frankly, when I arrived at the monastery Thursday evening,
I was not feeling tormented by my spiritual questions: I was
exhausted. I had packed bags for six children for a four-day
stay, and then the seven of us had left for the Gare de Lyon
to take the train to Nemours. A sister met us there in a
minivan to drive us to the monastery. In short, my interior
conflict had been buried underneath very mundane pre-
occupations and bodily fatigue. I was thinking of nothing
at all. We settled in for the night. We were put up in two
small cells separated by an oratory.

Friday morning, I woke up early. It was daylight. Since
the children were still sleeping, I went to the oratory. Upon
entering , I noticed a Byzantine cross at the back. To the
right of the cross there was a large icon of Mary, and to
the left, a painting of the Holy Face from the Shroud of
Turin, next to a window opening out on the sky. I walked
up and sat down. My gaze was very quickly drawn to
the painting of the Holy Face. Suddenly, I began to feel the
same chills that had come over me on the beach and in
my bedroom. I could sense in my skin that something was
going to happen. And suddenly, I saw the eyes of the Holy
Face open! And I plunged into an absolutely unspeakable
beatitude. Then, after a period of time that felt fairly long,
the eyes of the Holy Face closed again and things came
back to normal. I slowly came round and looked up at
the sky. Abruptly, I realized what had just happened and
was afraid. I felt that I was completely losing my mind.
I was terribly worried for my children. Having already

lost their mother, they would really suffer terribly if their
father were sent off to a psychiatric hospital. I wondered
what was happening to me; everything was a blur in my
head. It took me a very long time to come down to earth.

Then I turned my eyes back to the Holy Face. I had
decided I was not going to budge anymore. Even if the
children came in, I was not going to budge until I had
a clear answer. I had had enough of this hide-and-seek-
playing God! I could not put up with it any longer. I was
not a masochist. This time, it was do or die; I wanted it
all to end now. Then, His eyes opened again. And at that
precise moment, I was illuminated. I was turned totally
inside out. It was a complete reversal. At last! As incredible as it might seem, in one instant I had become ready
to throw away the Jewish Law. I no longer wanted to eat
kosher. It was the coup de grâce. I, an Orthodox Jew,
testify that without this grace, I would never have been
able to abandon the practice of the Law. I understand so
well what Saint Paul experienced in his flesh.

The first consequence of this illumination was a total
change in my frame of reference. Before, I had a desire
for Christ. Now, I had a loving faith in the very Person
of Jesus. Before, my references had been the Bible, the
Talmud, and the teachers I had had during my rabbinical
formation. I had tried to fit the Messiah into my talmudic
boxes or into my Jewish mystical categories, and if He did
not fit into them, I refused Him. Suddenly, He became
my reference, the foundation, the source of everything.
No theologian can convince someone to give up his way
of seeing the world—what he thinks, his values. There is
only grace. Father O. could not give me what Jesus alone
can give.

Next, I discovered Scripture in a new light. I understood
the Old Testament through Christ. The Church's Magisterium says that all the Scriptures speak but one word,

the Word. Now, when I read the Old Testament, I see the Word everywhere, and not only in the prophetic passages that announce the coming of Jesus. Indeed I see passages where a person had a relationship with the second Person of the Trinity. A number of passages in the New Testament attest to these relations with Jesus. For example, in Saint John's Gospel, Jesus said to the Pharisees: "Your father Abraham rejoiced that he was to see my day; he saw it and was glad" (8:56). Or again, Saint Peter, in the Acts of the Apostles, says of David: "He foresaw ... the resurrection of the Christ" (2:31). I recognized that all of Scripture speaks of God the Trinity. Yes, the Lord truly opened my mind to the Scriptures. As Saint Paul says, there was a veil before my eyes, and it had fallen. *Everything* became clear.

In Galatians 4, Paul reprimands the Galatians who have converted but want to submit to Jewish Law again. He does an allegorical and christological reading of the Jewish Law (see 21–31). He compares Hagar, Abraham's servant, and his wife, Sarah, to the two Covenants: the old one, that of Mount Sinai, and the new one, that of Jesus. Hagar, the first Covenant, brings slave children into the world; Sarah, the New Covenant, free children. A Jew, to be sure, could *not* accept this reading. This is why Paul says that Jews have a veil before their eyes when they read the Scriptures (see 2 Cor 3:14). I know it; I have had that experience. I now understand that the New Testament is in the Old as a son is in his mother. So long as he is in her womb, he cannot be seen. At his birth, so that he can live and grow, the cord has to be cut to separate him from his mother. Even so, he remains her son. He is going to bring something "new", working a rupture, and at the same time, he gives another dimension to his mother, renewing her. Thus the New Testament is born from the Old and brings something new, such as the Trinitarian God, who had not been clearly seen as the God who becomes flesh.

Finally, the last consequence of this illumination was that I felt called to become a servant of the Church. When I came out of the oratory, only one thing interested me: Him, Jesus, God become man! But I said nothing to anyone, to either the children or the sisters. I stayed very calm, and for the whole week I did not change anything in our way of life. I continued to eat kosher. It was on the evening of Shabbat, back at home, that the miracle took place. Like every Friday evening, I was starting the time switch so that the lights would go out on their own without my having to turn them off, since in the Jewish religion, you are not allowed to turn off the lights on the Shabbat. As usual, we were singing and eating our festive meal. It was then I got up to push the switch. I turned out the light. I was surprised myself by what I had just done—I who until then had been so scrupulous in respecting Jewish Law! I turned it back on right away. The children were looking at me, stupefied. I had them sit back down and explained myself. I explained by telling them my story with Jesus, from its beginnings.

From one day to the next there was no more Shabbat or kosher at home. It was finished! The children, who had always known me dressed as a rabbi, now saw me dressed like everybody: in jeans and a shirt or a tee shirt. You probably think they must have been shocked by this very quick change? Well, no actually, not at all: the way my conversion was accepted by my children, who had not been illuminated like me, was a miracle. For me there is no question about it. Likewise, the way I lived out these things myself was a grace. For my conversion might have been a shock for me too: I might have become disconnected from reality. But no, I got back to normal life and kept my feet on the ground. I was still a balanced man. The supernatural does not come to destroy the natural.

New Life

Sometimes I am asked what changed in my life with this conversion. In fact, at the beginning I wanted to become a priest, but it was gently explained to me that with seven children that was impossible. However it may be, I am called to serve the Church through the apostolate of preaching. "As each has received a gift, employ it for one another, as good stewards of God's varied grace: whoever speaks, as one who utters oracles of God; whoever renders service, as one who renders it by the strength which God supplies", writes Saint Peter in his first Letter (4:10–11). Everyone has his vocation. However, whatever the gift, we have received it in order to use it for the service of others. When I give a lesson, I always try to be of service to those listening to me.

What my conversion fundamentally changed was my way of living with others. The first change, notable for an Orthodox Jew: I was now sensitive to the suffering of all, even if they were not Jewish, and I prayed for all those entrusted to my prayer, even if I did not know them. I no longer saw others as goys, meaning non-Jews, or indifferent strangers. I had more tenderness for the other and awareness of the other, whoever he may be. This completely changed my attitude toward him.

At last the conflict that pitted my heart against my reason was behind me: I was totally ready to take the plunge.

I was baptized on September 14, 2008, the feast of the Triumph of the Cross, with the Sisters of Bethlehem, by total immersion in an enormous tub. I was dressed in a large white alb and completely soaked. At last! I was forty-three years old. It was my dear Father O. who baptized me in the name of the Father, and of the Son, and of the Holy Spirit, breathing an immense sigh of relief—or exhaustion! May God bless him!

My baptismal name is Jean-Marie Élie. For a long time I considered calling myself Paul, but I finally kept the first name Jean, the name my parents had given me, the name of my grandfather and my favorite evangelist. Do I need to explain why I chose the name Marie? As for Élie, this was the name given to me when I went to the Holy Land. Afterward I learned that the prophet Elijah was the founder of the Carmelites. Moreover, many converted Jews entered the Carmelites, for example, Saint Teresa Benedicta of the Cross (Edith Stein) and the German Jewish pianist Hermann Cohen. The founders of the Discalced Carmelites, Saint Teresa of Avila and Saint John of the Cross, descended from families of converted Jews.

A few months before my baptism, I met Pétronille, whom I had been advised to meet in order to verify whether my Jewish mysticism was "Catholic kosher". Pétronille confessed to me that she knew nothing about that, so we talked about *other* things. The following summer, when I was looking for a place to spend vacation with the children, someone suggested I bring them to Paray-le-Monial, a small town in Burgundy where the Sacred Heart of Jesus appeared to Saint Margaret Mary and where there are programs for families throughout the summer. We ran into Pétronille there! To get back to Paris, we took the same train, and she helped with some of my children, notably Gabriel, my little blond, who began to play the go-between. He told her: "Take care of us and Papa!" We were married, and three years later, in

January 2012, our son Nathanaël was born. Pétronille was forty-six, and he was her first child! A truly biblical story! Glory be to God! I would like to pay tribute to Pétronille, who is so cheerful and smiling and who committed herself to me and my family with full knowledge of the facts and was not afraid.

After my baptism, I called my brothers and sisters to invite them over to my house. I told them my story with Jesus from the very beginning. But they did not ask me questions about my conversion. They resented that I had not told them anything and reproached me for having cut myself off from the family through my successive decisions. I am sorry for this lack of understanding, and I would like to find a way to a real relationship with them again. I have never directly brought up the subject with my father, but I go to visit him regularly at La Courneuve with the children and Pétronille, whom he has made very welcome. On my phone, I keep a photo of Nathanaël on his grandfather's knees. They are both smiling. That makes me happy, for now my father is the only link I have left with my family and the Jewish community, which has banned me.

What Did My Children Say?

With hindsight, I think the greatest miracle of this whole story is what happened with the children. Of course the parents' choices have an influence on a child. But at heart, he makes his own choice. For example, I did not follow in my parents' footsteps. I thought that my children's fidelity to their mother's religion on the one hand, and on the other the education they had received in Lubavitcher schools and the practice of the Law that had filled their daily lives, would make my change very difficult. But the Lord heard the prayer I addressed to him on that momentous night.

In fact, each child followed his own spiritual path, at his own pace, as he saw fit. Youssef-Raphaël and Menahem were the first to ask for baptism. They were baptized in June 2009, one year after me, on the feast of the Holy Trinity. During the summer of 2009, all the children went away on vacation camp with L'Eau Vive (Living Water), a Catholic youth camp. Youssef-Raphaël, who was ten, asked to be confirmed there. I did not know beforehand: he told me about it himself on the telephone. Rachel was baptized in the Jordan on July 31, the feast of Saint Ignatius of Loyola, as part of a pilgrimage to the Holy Land during the same summer (2009). Myriam asked for baptism one year later, in August 2010. She received her First Communion and was confirmed at the same time. Menahem received the sacrament of confirmation during the summer of 2010.

At this time, Déborah and Rivka did not wish to be baptized. However, they did attend Mass with us. I asked them if they wanted to celebrate the Jewish feasts and Shabbat again, but they said no. They were not indifferent, but they have very high standards. Déborah attended a Foyer de Charité boarding school for four years. Each year, I gave her the option of switching to a public school, but she was not interested. She attended the beatification of John Paul II in Rome in May 2011. Finally, during her last school year at the Foyer school in Courset, in the month of November, she received a grace. God gave her a sign; that is what she said. She entered the Church during the Easter Vigil of 2012, that is, four years after my own baptism. Rivka is not baptized, but she wears a cross that she conceals when she goes to public school.

Obviously, my new life has had an influence on them. I would even say that is a blessing. This means that my transformation inspired their curiosity and made them interested. Nevertheless, they might very well have told me: "Dad, it's your path, not ours." Rivka did; she is free, and we are completely fine with that in the family. It does not pose any problems. Rivka remembers very well the moment I began to turn toward Christianity. She recalls the first time she saw the representation of the Virgin Mary in my room and says that she was not shocked by it. When I gave her the option of going to Talmud Torah classes, she refused. She believes in God, but not in Jesus Christ. Sometimes she prays to the Virgin Mary. The apparitions of the Virgin make her want to believe, but she is seeking proof. She says that if God wants her to be Christian, He only has to let her know. My children are very open and we talk about everything, even while they respect my authority.

I have asked myself if they feel guilty with respect to their mom. In all honesty, I have not wanted to bring up the subject with them directly. For their personal growth, I have not wanted them to be in constant mourning for their mother, even though each year we celebrate her departure to Heaven. The only one who has expressed a troubled conscience is Youssef. He was tormented. "Is Mom, in Heaven, okay with this?" he asked me one day. This did not prevent him from being the first one to want baptism.

We do not have a little chapel at home as in some Catholic families. I do not want a corner reserved for God because in reality there is no corner without God. We cook, work, and sleep in the hand of God. At our house, and this is something I have maintained from the Jewish tradition, the table is the altar. First of all, to be straightforward, it is more practical, because there at least, everyone comes together; there is no need to call them for an hour. We say the blessing and sometimes we do a bit of the Rosary. I say ten Hail Marys with my prayer intentions, and then each child says one with his own intentions. But I prefer the children to give pride of place to individual prayer, that is, to their personal relationship with Christ. Anyway each has a little prayer corner in his room with a statue and a cross. In the evening, I tell them: "Don't forget to say your prayers! Have you thanked God? Say a short prayer before going to sleep!" I motivate them, but without insisting, and I certainly do not go check.

I have asked my children if they feel my conversion has changed me as a person. Rivka says I am less stressed than before. She also thinks my faith is greater. According to her, my prayers were less profound and sincere before. Déborah was very moved by the fact that after my conversion I began forgiving others and in turn asking for forgiveness. I have taught them to ask for forgiveness and to forgive each other. Before we talked about forgiveness on Yom Kippur, but it was not the same. Youssef says I was more exacting when I was a religious Jew: I did not let anything go. Now, he thinks I am just as attentive, but with love. He also says I am more open. Becoming a Christian does not mean wanting to become perfect, like an Orthodox Jew. I live in God with my faults and my weaknesses. Today I am able to see myself as I am. This makes me less hard on others.

I too feel that I have changed. I am freer in relation to God, more at peace; I feel more natural with God—even though I am living through more difficult trials than when I was a practicing Jew. I am more confident, and it is God who gives me this confidence. With the difficulties I have encountered, which I will shortly address, I have lived through some excruciating periods. The children were surprised by my calm, by my serenity. For them, it was clear that Jesus was helping me. For that matter, I would like to thank here all of the people who have prayed for me and helped me in one way or another. I would especially like to thank my wife Pétronille, who has supported me unfailingly.

Since my conversion, I am also more joyful, with an interior joy. I live simply in His presence, even when I do not feel it. I want to help the poor, and I am sensitive to the sufferings of all peoples, not only the sufferings of the Jewish people. I pray for everyone, even for people with whom I share no emotional or communal bond. I have another view of the world, that of the non-Jew. This is very important to me. Look at Paul. When he was Saul, he had no non-Jewish friends. When he became Paul, he did. This is a radical change.

"Lord, Forgive Them, for They Know Not What They Do"

My conversion to Christ has done *a lot* of damage. Where there are graces, there is the cross. We see it in the life of Jesus: His own people did not accept Him, as Saint John says in his prologue to his Gospel (see Jn 1:11). In Judaism, this refusal has not changed. Times have changed, but the Jewish mentality on this particular point has remained the same. I am not saying this to accuse but rather to testify. I say it in peace because I feel at ease, at peace inside. I knew I would be misunderstood and violently rejected. This has been the case. I have received threatening letters, even blackmail. My best friends, friends for thirty years, rejected me from one day to the next. I no longer exist for them. I am dead.

My case is not exceptional. Saint Paul, Saint Peter, and so many others have gone through it. I was familiar with the story of Rabbi Drach. When in 1823 Paul Drach, the son-in-law of the chief rabbi of Paris, a brilliant mind destined for a bright career in Judaism, converted to Catholicism, he had serious troubles. His brother-in-law chased him out of the family home, and his wife disappeared with their three children. In every era, the conversion of a Jew to Christianity has been judged unacceptable in the heart of the Jewish people and has provoked violent reactions. On this point, I feel there is not much difference between Judaism and Islam. I am not saying this to throw stones at Judaism or to create hostility. In ·any case, hate for the converted Jew exists. I am saying so because this is part of my testimony. What the children and I have lived through—threats and acts of violence, as well as people refusing eye contact or staring violently—has affected us to the core. We are human beings; we are not without feelings.

Here, I am asking the Jewish community of France to respect my choice and let me live as a Christian. To this end I am calling upon all those community leaders and rabbis who are already aware or will be aware of my choice, and I am also asking that my children be left in peace. For my part, I bear no grudge, no violence or bitterness toward my Jewish blood brothers. Did not Saint Paul say: "For I could wish that I myself were accursed and cut off from Christ for the sake of my brethren, my kinsmen according to the flesh" (Rom 9:3)? They still remain brothers to me. I have not forgotten what I am by becoming a Christian: I am a Jew converted to Christ. I do not renounce anything that Judaism has given me or that I have been able to bring to Judaism. But I simply go on living in a different way.

CONCLUSION

Judaism and Christianity

To conclude, since I have lived the Old Covenant and am now living the New, I would like to clarify the most perceptible differences between Judaism and Christianity. As I said, there is both continuity and rupture between the Old and New Testaments.

Faith and the Law

Sometimes I am asked what distinguishes the Jewish faith from the Christian faith. Yet we do not speak of Jewish faith because in Judaism, what is put into practice is the Law. The Christian system consists of faith in Christ; the Jewish system consists of the Law of Moses. This does not mean there is no faith among Jews, for there certainly is, but faith is much less in the foreground, because what is essential is the practice of the Law.

Furthermore, in Judaism God does not encounter a man but a people. This might seem theoretical but it changes everything in daily life. Judaism is built around the notion of a people and not of individuals. Among Jews, it is the people who is elect; among Christians, each man, woman, and child is elect. On Mount Sinai, God addresses the Hebrew people through the intermediary of Moses, but He does not come to speak to each person individually. It is true that God addresses Abraham personally. But

Abraham is not the great man of Judaism, much less so than for Christians. The absolute reference is Moses, who transmitted the Law and is the founder of Judaism. Christ, however, goes to meet persons, one by one. He calls each one where he is, and where he is in his life: Simon Peter, the Samaritan woman, Mary Magdalene, Zacchaeus, me, you. It is after this encounter that individuals desire to put themselves at the service of the collective. In Christianity, God looks at me, and through this look, He gives me His love and His graces. This merciful look lifts me up and makes me better. In my experience, you cannot love the "we"—others, the universal human community—until you are in a relationship of love with God. It is written in the Talmud that the cause of the destruction of the second Temple and of the dispersal of the Jews outside of the Holy Land by the Romans happened because there was no love among the people. According to some rabbis, the construction of the third Temple will be achieved only through gratuitous love.

Certainly, it is written in the Law that Jews have the obligation to love God with all their hearts. This is spoken about, written about, read about, but it is very difficult to put into concrete practice because what is important is the Law. Certainly, there is the commandment to love God, but can love be commanded? Love is not imposed. Love is proposed through love. And it is by becoming aware of God's love for me in the events of my life that I desire to be faithful to Him and to love Him.

Perfection or Grace

When I was a religious Jew, I did not believe that God loved me as I was. Now that I am a Christian, I do. Even

though the Christian must try to become better, he does
not count upon his human strength to do so. The Christian's effort must focus on the time he spends with God,
those encounters with God in which he seeks to enter into
relationship with Him. For we know that it is His grace
that transforms us, on condition that we let this grace act.
In Judaism, if I may say so, I slogged away. I could be
justified through my own strength and my merit, even
though I believed that God was helping me. The Christian
believes that God works in him. His role is to let Him act.
I know now that our wills are weak; thus we must live
above all through our loyal faith. In Judaism, I was seeking
perfection. In Christ, I do not seek perfection through my
own effort. As Jesus said to Paul, who was complaining
about his weakness: "My grace is sufficient for you, for my
power is made perfect in weakness" (2 Cor 12:9). Imperfections are not something to worry about, but to accept
humbly, in the knowledge that God acts through them
mysteriously. Accepting yourself as you are, with your
faults, your wounds, your weaknesses—which can be a
heavy cross to bear—and believing that God uses them to
bring other souls to Him, this is something I never learned
in Judaism.

And because it is Jesus who acts in us, Jesus can reveal
Himself to whomever he wishes, even to the littlest ones,
like Saint Margaret Mary or Marthe Robin, who was in
no way extraordinary, who was simple and who received
thousands of people in the room where she was bedridden.
He also addresses great sinners such as Augustine, Francis
of Assisi, Ignatius of Loyola, and Charles de Foucauld. In
Judaism, for God to reveal Himself to a man, he must be
pure, wise, trained in mysticism, scrupulous in the application of the Laws. Recall the condescending words of
the people from Jesus' own country after being taught by

Jesus in their synagogue: "Is not this the carpenter's son?" (Mt 13:55).

Certainly, the Bible tells how God heals a foreign widow and a Persian dignitary. But the Jews were scandalized by these healings. I repeat, for it is essential: in Judaism, it is not believed that God might speak to each person. In the Church, yes, God can really speak to me during prayer, even if, to be sure, the words that I hear have to be verified. Great saints like Teresa of Avila spoke about this at length. As Pope Benedict XVI said during a prayer vigil for life in Advent (November 27, 2010): "The Lord embraces us all in his love that saves and consoles." I have never heard a chief rabbi talk like that. And yet, I am not a greatly emotional person, and Benedict XVI even less so.

For God or in God

Before His Passion, Jesus said to His apostles: "No longer do I call you servants ... but I have called you friends" (Jn 15:15). This is the difference I have experienced: Jesus calls us all into friendship with Him. And today, now that I am a Christian, I can live this deep friendship with Him even though I am a sinner. Even more, as Saint Paul says, Jesus is our big brother (see Heb 2:11). God is our brother! This is unthinkable in Judaism, according to which, every evening, we are judged while we sleep. God judges our souls, and if the scales fall on the right side we can go on living to accumulate points by practicing the Law. When one is Jewish, there is no relationship of intimacy and friendship with God in daily life, except those of a few great, just persons mentioned in the holy books. Jesus calls us *all* to participate in His divine life, to live in Him

as He lives in us, to change our natural lives into supernatural lives, to divinize our lives though a link to God:
it is totally crazy! God became man so that man might
become God, wrote Saint Irenaeus in the second century
and Saint Athanasius in the fourth. Just as the consecrated
bread is His Body, when we eat the consecrated Host, we
become His Body. God invites us to become "partakers of
the divine nature" (2 Pet 1:4). In Judaism, it is different: I
perform acts for God. But I do not participate *in a real way*
in His divine life. Jesus said: "Abide in me, and I in you"
(Jn 15:4). The essential thing is this relationship with God.

Yearly Forgiveness or Daily Forgiveness

My children have made me notice that I am more inclined
to forgive now. Naturally, forgiveness exists in Judaism.
But it is only fully lived in Christ, who asks us to forgive
the same offense committed by the same person seventy
times seven times (see Mt 18:22). That is to say, I must try
tirelessly to forgive someone who does me wrong every
day. But I cannot forgive by my own strength. Some things
are humanly unforgivable. As Jesus said: "[A]part from me
you can do nothing" (Jn 15:5). Here is another big difference from Judaism: as a Christian, if I manage to forgive, I
do not take any pride in it—I know that it does not come
from me; I have given it my good will, but it is the grace
of God that acts in me. This comes from Jesus, who says on
the Cross: "Father, forgive them; for they know not what
they do" (Lk 23:34). When you have experienced God's
forgiveness through confession, you understand many
things, and enter into the logic of mercy toward others.

Once a year at Yom Kippur, Jews ask forgiveness for
the whole year. For example, I would send an apology or

receive a letter from someone asking my forgiveness for a trick he had played on me. But during the year, nothing on the order of forgiveness would happen. Asking forgiveness or forgiving once a year is not enough. Jesus leads us further! Forgiving is a way of life from day to day. Jesus says, before going to see Him, at Mass for example, if you have a conflict with your brother, go find him and come back to see Him afterward (see Mt 5:23–24). Jesus asks us to go so far as to forgive our enemies and to love them. This idea is entirely foreign to Judaism: you hate your enemies. Of course, it is humanly impossible to love our enemies, but God in us makes us able to desire their well-being and to forgive them—which does not keep us from affirming our views and fighting for them.

Thanks be to God I have never had difficulty confessing, even though this practice was foreign to me. The priest does not judge me; he gives me God's forgiveness. Jesus said: "I did not come to judge the world but to save the world" (Jn 12:47). It is wonderful: you can confess to any priest, you can say everything, and you are forgiven. I had never been able to talk about intimate things with a rabbi. It is very important to be able to unburden yourself, in all confidence, in order to walk with God and in God, with your sinful humanity. The rabbi's gaze is totally different from that of the priest. Jews do not unburden themselves to the rabbi with an open heart for fear of being judged by the community.

Persecution

I am well aware that Christians or persons bearing the Christian name have done wrong to the Jewish people, for example, wanting to convert them by force by threatening them with death. And John Paul II's gesture of repentance was tremendous and exemplary. Of course, members of the Church behaved wrongly, but there were also many who did wonderful things for the Jews of Europe. It is enough to go to Yad Vashem in Jerusalem to see this. The police captain who saved my mother's family was a goy. And how did American Jews behave toward their European Jewish brothers during the war? I am not trying to be polemical, but relations between Jews and Christians must be founded on freedom of speech and on the truth.

And I also cannot ignore the sufferings of my first Jewish brothers converted to Christ who suffered martyrdom at the hands of their own Jewish brothers. It is not for me to judge them; I am not God. It is for me to forgive. But look at how, in our day, Israeli Jews converted to Christ are obliged to conceal themselves, and yet Israel is a democratic society. As I have already said, even today, Jews pray a nineteenth blessing that was added to the chief eighteen-blessing prayer. And this prayer is in fact a curse on Jews who have converted to Christ. In the twenty-first century, three times a day Jews still curse Jews who have become Christians, and I am not supposed to say so? No, I am not ashamed of my conversion. Some desire to cast guilt on me because I have renounced my people, but I am not renouncing anything or anyone. Moreover I am very well aware that if tomorrow another Hitler came to power, I would have to hide, because converted Jew or not, I would be hunted down.

The Community or the World

Mother Teresas do not exist in Judaism. In Christianity, the notion of service is central. Each Christian must be a servant, as Jesus exemplified by washing the feet of His disciples on the eve of His death. In Orthodox Judaism, you do not find women or men who go freely into the slums to take care of anybody, irrespective of religion, just to bring love, compassion, and comfort. This is because the emphasis is much more on the relationship to the Law than on the relationship between persons. Despite his high birth and learning, Saint Paul said he had become a servant of all for Christ. He could have enjoyed great honor if he had remained Jewish. I have never heard a rabbi tell me to become my brother's servant. This does not mean there is no mutual help among Jews. But Jesus asks more of us than to help our close neighbors and those we love. The pagans too give each other help within the same family or clan.

Man cannot live without love. His life is deprived of meaning if he does not receive the revelation of love and does not encounter God's love for him. In ultra–Orthodox Judaism, I did not experience this loving gaze. It is true that Jews try to apply the commandment "Thou shalt love thy God." But since the emphasis is not put on a personal loving relationship with God, this commandment cannot be lived concretely.

In becoming a Christian, I learned how to love the other as he is and not only because he is a member of my community. This was a revolution, an interior rebirth; it gave me a new way of seeing, a new heart, and new feelings. Today I am sensitive to world events, to all events and not only those that affect the Jewish people, and I pray for the world with all my heart. I pray when there are individuals suffering throughout the world. I never had this awareness as a Jew. I was not educated to have that awareness. There was only awareness of the Jewish people and of Israel, even if from time to time, you might pray for the country you live in or those governing it. But praying spontaneously as a family for those who are suffering is just not done. I now have this grace of loving everyone, without being selective. In Judaism you learn to love Jews and to look upon others as wanting to harm Jews. I am sorry to have to say so, but this has been my experience.

What other religion says you must love your enemies? What other religion says that God, because He loves me, suffers for me, like a mother? Christ, not Judaism, teaches me to love sinners, even though it is true that some Jews today are trying to bring their nonbelieving Jewish brothers back to God. To love every man you need the grace of God; otherwise, it is impossible! My conversion changed the way I look at others. Put differently, when I was a practicing Jew, God was Law and the Law separated the pure from the impure, pure people from impure people. The God revealed by Christ is love, and love welcomes the other as he is.

For Saul, God only heard the prayers of Jews; for Paul, God is there for all and hears everyone. A barrier, a form of protectionism, has fallen. The same has happened for me. For example, when Jewish children died in an atrocious killing in Toulouse in March 2012, I prayed for them and their families, but I also prayed for the three Roma girls and the children who lost their soldier father in the days before. Jesus removed the wall of hate between Jews and Gentiles; Paul told us so. Thus, we should pray for each other. We Christians must be above the fray, because we are no longer of the world. We must carry the message of love and pray for all—irrespective of race, condition, and religion.

Codified Prayer or Spontaneous Prayer

In Christianity, everyone can experience interior silence with God and in God, during Mass or a retreat, or in the secrecy of his room. In Judaism, I never heard anyone talk about a personal relationship with God in interior silence. God is talked about through theology and textual exegesis, but God is studied as a scientific object. For that matter some Christians can make the same mistake. For the Word of God to transform us—and it can transform us, *in a real way*—we have to maintain a relationship with it that is less intellectual, more vital, and I would say, like a love affair. We must realize that this Word gives life, that it nourishes us in the strongest sense, like food for the soul. But this can be realized only when in silence we let grace work in us. Jewish prayer is different from this silent mental prayer to which Christ invites us. It is not the comprehension of a theme in a text that makes me grow in love for others or for God. Having your head stuck only in theology does not make you grow in love. Theology is at the service of contemplation. Saint Thomas Aquinas' example in this area is magnificent.

Is It Easier to Be a Jew or a Christian?

Many Jews think I was looking for the easy way out in becoming a Christian. They think I cracked because it was too hard raising six children alone, or because I was psychologically fragile and needed to catch my breath, to try something new. Because of my supernatural revelations, they say it all comes from my imagination. But I have my two feet firmly on the ground; I am not up in a cloud. I continue to suffer and to live through trials and an intense spiritual battle in regard to faith, as every Christian does. Frankly, in the face of the troubles I have had because of my conversion, which have cut me off from my community and my roots, and seeing how the Church is viewed today,

I have not taken the easy way out. It seems to me that Peter, John, Stephen, and Paul did not take the easy way out by following Christ after His death!

Here, I have to admit that I feel nostalgic toward a communal way of life—not communitarianism, which encloses and excludes, but the community of life that provides warmth, gives roots, teaches, nourishes, and sends its members out into the world. In the parishes I have known, I have not found this community life. I know it exists in a few places, but it is all too rare. At the end of prayer at the synagogue, for example, drinks are offered. A Christian alone is a Christian in danger. Often it is not even enough to have a Christian family. Teenagers hungry for social interaction and friendships especially need a fraternal community. From the outside, the Jewish Laws appear constraining. But Christian life, if we want to live it fully, is yet more crucifying and more exacting on the human level, because love requires us to go beyond ourselves continually; it engages the whole being, and this is not required in order to the practice the Law.

When a Christian is living through a dark period in his soul, feeling anguished, empty, it is like being obliterated. There is nothing to hold onto if not Jesus, yet in those moments the Christian often does not feel Him. A Jew always has the practice of the Law to cling to; it gives a rhythm to each hour of his day, like the steps of a ladder. The Christian has no ladder: he has only the arms of Jesus, which raise him up like an elevator, to borrow the metaphor of Saint Thérèse of the Child Jesus. My entire relation to God came through the practice of the Law. Now that I am Christian, I have a personal relationship with God. But when for whatever reason this relationship is veiled, when I am unable to feel the presence of God, I no longer have anything to hold onto that is perceptible and concrete like the minute daily practice of Judaism. Being Christian has allowed me to come face-to-face with myself, to see myself as I am, so weak. There is only He and I. In Judaism, the Law intervenes. You are never face-to-face with yourself in your nakedness and destitution. You face not yourself but the Law, which you apply and which risks filling you with pride because you think you are better than others.

The Christian's whole relationship to God is founded on tenderness and love. When the Christian no longer feels the love or tenderness of God on the human level—and it happens a lot (just look at Mother Teresa's fifty years of interior night)—he has nothing to grab hold of but his will's act of faith in God's love, whereas the Jew clings to the Law. It is harder being a Christian than being a Jew, because it is harder to love than to follow a Law.

Since I became a Christian, I am also more exposed to danger because the barrier of the Law and the community ghetto no longer protects me from temptations. Before I lived in a bubble. Of course a Jew has temptations, but since he lives in a ghetto, he has fewer of them. He does not really form bonds of friendship with goys because they are considered impure. He keeps his distance from them. And then the community protects him: the community keeps a very close watch on each of its members. You know you are being watched, like a child by his parents. Becoming a Christian is like becoming an adult. There is no one directly telling us to do this or that every minute of the day and condemning us if we do the wrong thing. This is why it is much harder being Christian: you are free!

A Jew can live in France like a foreigner uninvolved in what happens in the country around him. He can make himself immune from the challenges posed by the world outside his community. The Law and the community form an invisible shell around him and protect him from everything that is impure. He is much less exposed to outside influences. But as a result he does not grow in humility. Perhaps it is because of this that the practicing Jew is sometimes arrogant. But this also happens to Christians who rely only on their own strength or those who have received great graces and forget that their gifts come from God. Catholics can behave like Jews in the application of the moral law. Yet Saint Paul said that the Lord told him: "My grace is sufficient for you, for my power is made perfect in weakness" (2 Cor 12:9). In a mysterious way, God makes use of our weaknesses and faults.

The God of Moses and the God of Jesus

There is a tendency to think that the God of the Jews is the same as the God of the Christians. Yes, of course—and no, not at all: it depends on one's point of view. A Trinitarian God is inconceivable in Judaism, or a God who comes to me in my sinful humanity, or a God who becomes man and says that He came not to be served but to serve, or a God who dies out of love for me and says: "I did not come to judge the world but to save the world" (Jn 12:47). I am rambling, but this saying by Jesus is inconceivable for an Orthodox Jew as is a God who loves me and takes me as I am with my lacks, my temptations, my faults, and my repeated failings, or a God who respects my freedom to choose and does not force himself upon me.

The idea of a God who loved me first before I did anything at all for Him is unfamiliar to Jews, even if He revealed Himself in places in the Bible. In Judaism, for God to love me, I must conform to the letter of the Law, and the more I practice the Law the more I am loved by God.

It is quid pro quo. For that matter, there are Christians who are stuck on that idea. They have not integrated Jesus' good news that God loves us as a father loves his children. With the Christian God, I have discovered another God, a God who loves me for what I am—which does not of course excuse me from leading a moral life since moral rules are the school of love. This is the whole meaning of Saint Augustine's "Love and do what you will." Once you are living in love, external laws no longer need to be applied; you have already internalized them. Thus, going to Mass is no longer an obligation but a vital necessity flowing out of love.

As Saint Paul said, I boast in my weaknesses because I know that God acts in my imperfections. He does not need me to be perfect in order to act in me and to transform me body, soul, and spirit by His love. It is hard to understand this because we have been educated, even in secular schools, in merit. I am insisting on this point so that we fully understand just how radical Christ's revolution is, but I do not want to oppose Judaism and Christianity because Jesus never did so. Jesus was opposed to legalistic behavior. As I was saying earlier, it seems to me that Christianity is to Judaism what a son is to his mother. He will always remain his mother's son and will honor her, but in order for him to live, he must separate himself from her. Only then can the son bring forth something new.

Even though my Jewish brothers tell me that I have lost my way, I prefer my new life to the old, which was more reassuring but less true. Since my baptism, the Holy Spirit has brought forth His fruits in me: love, joy, peace, kindness, faith, and freedom. I have lived through trials and will live through others. I know that I will continue to sin, as this is part of the human condition, but I also know that our God, who is so like a father, will always be there to pick me up again, to forgive me, and to love me. That is the essential thing. In conclusion I would like to offer you a prayer by my big brother Saint Paul, who was set aflame by Jesus and who said yes to Him, renouncing his certitudes and his enviable social status. I make my own this prayer, which invites us to believe that God can achieve infinitely more in us than we can imagine. He wants to give us infinitely more than we ask:

> I bow my knees before the Father, from whom every family in heaven and on earth is named, that according to the riches of his glory he may grant you to be strengthened with might through his Spirit in the inner man, and that Christ may dwell in your hearts through faith; that you, being rooted and grounded in love, may have power to comprehend with all the saints what is the breadth and length and height and depth, and to know the love of Christ which surpasses knowledge, that you may be filled with all the fullness of God.
>
> Now to him who by the power at work within us is able to do far more abundantly than all that we ask or think, to him be glory in the Church and in Christ Jesus to all generations, for ever and ever. Amen. (Eph 3: 14–21)

MEDITATIONS INSPIRED BY
SAINT JOHN OF THE CROSS

O Jesus, O my Jesus, O my God,
As I have told You, O my Jesus, my love will
    be total, in fullness,
Not only when my soul leaves my body and
    the old man,
But even more so when, through the grace of
    Your Resurrection,
I will be resurrected by You and in You!
And yet, O Jesus, how good You are,
How infinite is Your goodness,
For this imperfect love that I give You,
This imperfect relation, given my human
    condition,
Refreshes You!
It is a joy for You!
How crazy that is, O my God!
I have wounded You and I have refreshed
    You!
This love I show You in my contemplation, in
    my adoration,
But also throughout my day, in my daily activ-
    ities, wounds You,
Wounds You with love for me.
Thus, O Jesus, behold our mutual cross:
I, I am wounded by love for You
And You, You are wounded by love for me!
Amen.

Your wood, which is this glorious Cross,
This divine throne,
This divine power with its charms that are
Love
Forgiveness
Grace
Wisdom
Reconciliation
Ransom.
Just as the life and roots of every tree is wood
And as man is a tree in the fields,
Just so, O Jesus, I have my life in You and my
    roots in You,
From this wood of the Cross.

I tenderly and joyfully kiss the Cross, Your throne, from which You saw, in full agony, what is happening in me, from this Cross, from which springs forgiveness, gratuitous love, freedom. Divine Lord! I love You unto madness, Jesus, because You are Jesus!

In contemplating the Cross of Christ, may we hear Jesus Himself murmuring in the depths of our hearts: "I love you, I love you My brother, I love you My sister, I love you infinitely. You are worth more than the evil you have done. Have no fear, I am here, My Cross protects you. Rise up, and look at Me on My Cross, gaze at Me on My Cross, contemplate Me on My Cross, venerate Me, adore Me. I give Myself to you, take Me. Take Me and walk in the shadow of My Cross."

By looking at You on Your Cross, O my God and My Savior Jesus, may I discover Your confidence, may I agree to discover You and to recognize You as He who alone can save us and make of our lives something great and beautiful.

May we let ourselves be grasped by Your love! And if each of us agrees regularly to take a few moments to contemplate the Cross of Christ, mystery of love, mystery of salvation, I am sure our lives will be transformed, because each of us would then feel that You, Jesus, are looking at him, enveloping him, and accompanying him tenderly, mercifully, lovingly.

ACKNOWLEDGMENTS

I would like to thank members of the Church, priests and laity who from the beginning and each in his own way have supported me through prayer, by giving advice, by trusting me, and by giving me a chance to teach. And I am asking forgiveness in advance from those whose names have escaped me.

With all my heart I give thanks to Georges Cardinal Cottier, O.P.; Brother Y., Carmelite; Father Pierre Fricot, Serviteur de la Parole, and to Sister Claire Pattier; Bishop Michel Aupetit; Fathers Christian Lancray-Javal, Patrick Faure, Pierre-Henri Montagne; Bishop Albert-Marie de Monléon; Fathers Jean-Pierre Gay, Jean-Pierre Billard, Charles Troesch, Michel Bernard, Marie-Michel (Carmel de Marie Vierge Missionnaire), Daniel Ange (Jeunesse Lumière), Benoit Domergue; Abbé Chouanard; Fathers Emmanuel Dumont, Vincent Bedon, Aguila (with his John Paul II fraternity in Fréjus), Alain Bandelier (Foyer de Charité); Abbé Loiseau; Brother Marie-Angel.

I also would like to thank Professor André Clément; the Little Sisters of Bethlehem and the lay members of Bethlehem; the Little Sisters of the Consolation of Draguignan; the Benedictine Sisters of Argentan; the Sisters of the Annunciation; the Foyer de Charité of Courset; the Brothers and Sisters of the Community of Saint John; Thierry and Anne Lefer; Marie-Thérèse Huguet; Catherine and Thierry Useldinger; Marie and Jean-Baptise Maillard; Marie-Noëlle and François Fihol; Dorothée and Claude Ribeyre; Nathalie and Arnaud Bouthéon; Juliette

Poulon; Sylvia Fenech; Annie Tardos; Myriam Fourchaud; the Emmanuel Community, especially Agnès and Jean de Chillaz; Inès and Laurent Mortreuil; and Corinne and Gilles de Craecker.

And of course, thanks to my very dear spiritual brother and father Bishop Michel Santier.

KEY DATES IN MY LIFE

June 10, 1964	Birth in Paris
1969 (age 5)	Move to Courneuve
1972 (age 8)	Attraction to the crucifix in Brittany; Jesus is my best friend
1976 (age 12)	Escapade at Sacré-Cœur in Montmartre, then First Communion
1979 (age 15)	I decide to convert
1982 (age 18)	I leave for Israel/the Holy Land
1987 (age 23)	Ultra-Orthodox Jew; rabbinical formation
1989 (age 25)	Return to France
1990 (age 26)	First marriage, then return to the Holy Land with my wife (for 18 months)
1994 (age 30)	Return to France; my first child, a girl!
July 2002	Death of my mother
December 2002	My first wife becomes sick
March 11, 2004	Death of my first wife
2007 (age 43)	Lustiger gives me a sign
2008 (age 44)	Coup de grâce, illumination

September 14, 2008	My baptism
2009 (age 45)	Marriage with Pétronille
January 3, 2012 (age 48)	Nathanaël's birth